THE
ETERNAL
COVENANT

Ralph A. Smith, *The Eternal Covenant: How the Trinity Reshapes Covenant Theology*
© 2003 by Ralph A. Smith

Published by Canon Press, P.O. Box 8729, Moscow, ID 83843
800-488-2034 / www.canonpress.org
Printed in the United States of America.

Cover design by Paige Atwood.

03 04 05 06 07 08   9 8 7 6 5 4 3 2 1

Library of Congress Cataloging-in-Publication Data

Smith, Ralph Allan.
  The eternal covenant : how the Trinity reshapes covenant theology /
Ralph Allan Smith.
      p. cm.
Includes bibliographical references.
  ISBN 1-59128-012-5 (pbk.)
  1. Covenant theology. 2. Trinity. I. Title.
  BT155.S615 2003
  231.7'6—dc21
                                          2003002349

THE ETERNAL
COVENANT

HOW THE TRINITY RESHAPES COVENANT THEOLOGY

Ralph A. Smith

CANON PRESS ▪ MOSCOW, IDAHO

THIS BOOK IS DEDICATED to my firstborn son, Ben Zedek, with prayer that God will bless him and enable him to fulfill the meaning of his name that he may be faithful to his Lord (Deut. 10:12–13).

Contents

Acknowledgments

This essay was originally provoked by a comment made by James Jordan in a lecture or perhaps an essay—I no longer remember the source. He said something to the effect that Reformed theologians had often seen the covenant as a trinitarian pact. The comment struck me because in my own reading of Reformed theology, I had not noticed the "trinitarian" aspect of the covenant. The substance of what Jim said remained with me for years, but it was only recently that I took time to look into it. Even more than that single comment, I am indebted to Jim's various publications and his emphasis on the Trinity for my own orientation to the subject. What I have written here is in some respects simply my reflection on his views. I am also indebted to him for interaction and encouragement through email.

Jeffrey J. Meyers, a Reformed minister and a specialist in the theology of the Trinity, has been generous in recommending books and discussing the Trinity in email correspondence. Jeff is perhaps the most well-read trinitarian theologian in the conservative Reformed world today, and his four lectures on the Trinity delivered at the Twelfth Annual Biblical Horizons Bible Conference were extremely helpful.

Finally, I also owe special thanks to Peter Leithart, who read an earlier version of this essay and offered helpful criticism. I am sure the final product is much better thanks to Peter's help, but the faults that remain are not his responsibility.

Doug Jones from Canon Press encouraged me to change the title into something more manageable and supplied the subtitle. My wife suggested the present title. She has also taught me more about God than all my other teachers.

Introduction

The most illustrious names in the history of Reformed theology have affirmed a covenant relationship between the Father and the Son, and not a few have specifically affirmed a relationship among all three persons of the Trinity. While there are differences of opinion among these theologians, it has been common to assume some sort of covenant between the Father and the Son for the redemption of God's elect. For a few, the covenant is almost a *theological* notion; for the vast majority, it is more properly considered "anthropological" since it is oriented to redemption and commonly linked with the idea of a covenant of works granted to Adam in the garden. The covenant with Adam is considered to be a covenant in which Adam merits blessing on the basis of his works, though most writers acknowledge the goodness of God in the covenant arrangement. What is remarkable is that the covenant with Adam, though in conception lower and in time later than the covenant between the Father and the Son, tends to be the paradigmatic covenant. The covenant between the Father and the Son is modeled after the covenant with Adam, and even though both the covenant of redemption and the covenant of grace are conceived of as taking place in the eternal counsel of God, the covenant of grace is often referred to as a "second covenant," the Adamic covenant being first.

The notion of a covenant among the persons of the Trinity is relevant not only to Reformed theology but, as the discussion of the covenant in Karl Barth makes clear,[1] relevant to the whole modern

---

[1] On the one hand, Barth recognizes the importance of the covenant for the doctrine of creation and redemption: "The decisive anchorage of the recognition that creation and covenant belong to

discussion of the Trinity. As we shall show here, already the Puritans addressed important issues that have to do with the interpersonal relations among Father, Son, and Spirit, and for at least some of the Dutch Reformed theologians, the covenant functioned as more than a mere means of salvation. As we shall also show, however, in Reformed theology, discussion of the covenant among the persons of the Godhead is fragmented, and its importance for the doctrine of the Trinity has been largely neglected. In part, that is because of differences among Reformed theologians about the nature of the covenant relationship in God, some in the Dutch Reformed tradition offering a significantly differing view from that of the Scottish Presbyterian tradition. While it would be wrong to characterize this as a question of whether or not a particular view is true to Reformed theology, it would be naïve to ignore the fact that these are issues with far-reaching consequences. For if there is a covenant relationship among the persons of the Trinity, it—not the covenant of works—ought to constitute the paradigmatic covenant

---

each other is the recognition that God the Creator is the triune God, Father, Son, and Holy Spirit. . . . The recognition of the unity of the divine being and its particularity as Father, Son, and Holy Spirit will prove effective in all these directions for the recognition not only of the interconnexions but also of the variations in the relation between creation and covenant" (*Church Dogmatics* [Edinburgh: T&T Clark, 1958], 3:48–49). On the other hand, although he sees that the purpose of creation and redemption is found in man being brought into covenantal union with God, Barth denies as clearly as he ever denies or affirms anything that there is or can be a covenant among the persons of the Trinity: "The thought of a purely inter-trinitarian decision as the eternal basis of the covenant of grace may be found both sublime and uplifting. But it is definitely much too uplifting and sublime to be a Christian thought." The reason for this unusually dogmatic denial seems to be found a few sentences later in the words: "How can even the most perfect decision in the bosom of the Godhead, if the Godhead remains alone, be the origin of the covenant, if it is made in the absence of the one who must be present as the second partner at the institution of the covenant to make it a real covenant, that is, man? To unite God in His attitude to man—whether in respect of His properties, or as Father, Son and Holy Spirit—there is no need of any particular pact or decree. God would not be God if He were not God in this unity" (*Church Dogmatics* [Edinburgh: T&T Clark, 1956], 4:66). Barth's solution to the basic questions posed by covenant theology is a failure worse than that of Cocceius, whose views he criticizes, but he is correct to point out that the traditional Reformed view is dualistic and that it errs in making the covenant of grace secondary to the covenant of works (ibid., 66). But since the anthropological orientation of the trinitarian covenant in Barth is even more radical than in orthodox Reformed theology, he has undermined his attempt to make the Trinity the true center of theology, though his doctrine of the Trinity is itself suspect along with many other aspects of his theology.

and therefore supply not only the key notion of systematic as well as biblical theology, but also the essential link between these two disciplines. Indeed, it should be the very center of the whole Christian worldview.

There are three basic questions that must be answered. Is there a covenantal relationship among the persons of the Trinity? What is the nature of that relationship? What are the implications of such a covenant? The first question determines our view of the ultimate source of the covenant. The second question determines the direction of our covenantal thought. The answer that we give to it will decide how the doctrine of the trinitarian covenant will affect our theology in general and its application to life. The third question is too broad to deal with adequately here, but we can suggest some of the implications that should be drawn as an introduction to the further development of the doctrine.

1

Is There a Covenant in the Trinity?

The history of the Reformed doctrine of a covenant among the persons of the Trinity is complicated by numerous issues, not the least of which is the fact that the covenant has often been thought of as a covenant between the Father and the Son, with little or no mention of the Holy Spirit, a discrepancy so great that Herman Hoeksema can refer to it as an implicit, albeit unintentional, denial of the Trinity.[1] In addition to the place that the Holy Spirit is thought to occupy in the covenant, there are questions about the relationship between this covenant and the covenant of works, about whether Christ enters this covenant as representative for His people or whether there is a second covenant between God and the elect in addition to the covenant with Christ, and about the relationship of this covenant to the doctrine of the decree. Not discussed by Reformed theologians, but nevertheless relevant, is the question of *perichoresis* as it relates to the notion of the covenant. We will discuss only a few of these issues, but in preparation for that discussion, we will begin with a brief survey of Reformed opinion on the covenant among the persons of the Trinity. What is most interesting from the perspective of this essay is the fact that so many Reformed theologians do recognize that the persons of the Trinity from eternity relate to one another in covenant. Given this fact, we need to investigate why it should be that the doctrine of the covenant is seldom seen to be grounded in this trinitarian relationship.

[1] Herman Hoeksema, *Reformed Dogmatics* (Grand Rapids: Reformed Free Publishing Association, 1966), 293.

REFORMED OPINION

While the majority of Reformed theologians and thinkers believe in some sort of covenant among the persons of the Trinity, there are exceptions, the most prominent of which is John Murray. Murray denies that there is a covenant with Adam in the garden of Eden, preferring instead to see the notion of a divine covenant as *essentially redemptive*, assuming that the word should be defined by its common use in Scripture (Gen. 6, 9, 12, etc.). If the word *covenant* is not used in Scripture for a particular arrangement, Murray does not call it a covenant, even if it seems otherwise to have the qualities of a covenant. But both Murray's denial of a covenant of works and the implicit denial of a pretemporal covenant are more a matter of language than substance. For just as Murray speaks of the Adamic "administration," in terms which will appear to many readers to be, for all intents and purposes, a "covenantal administration," so also he speaks of an "inter-trinitarian economy of salvation,"[2] which could be designated an "inter-trinitarian covenant" without being unjust to the content.

Another well-known Reformed theologian, O. Palmer Robertson, explicitly denies the covenant of redemption.[3] But considering the proportion of Reformed thinkers in favor of a covenant among the persons of the Trinity, one would have thought that Robertson would feel bound to explain and defend his position more than he does, especially since he is not simply following Murray. His approach seems to be that of Old Testament biblical theology, and it is not clear that he has given adequate thought to the issue from the perspective of systematic or even New Testament biblical theology. His definition of the covenant—a bond in blood sovereignly administered[4]—excludes the possibility of a trinitarian covenant. But

---

[2] *Systematic Theology,* vol. 2 of *Collected Writings of John Murray* (Edinburgh: Banner of Truth, 1977). On the Adamic administration, see 49–50. On the covenant of redemption, see 130–31.

[3] O. Palmer Robertson, *The Christ of the Covenants* (Grand Rapids: Baker, 1980), 53–54. In his lectures on the doctrine of the Trinity in twentieth century history, Jeff Meyers suggests—I believe correctly—that at least part of the reason for Robertson's rejection of the traditional notion of a covenant among the persons of the Trinity is to be found in the fact that he is interacting with the Scottish tradition and its notion of a pact or contract. Jeff J. Meyers, "The Trinity in Recent Theology, Lecture 4" in *2002 Biblical Horizons Bible Conference* (Niceville, Fla.: Biblical Horizons).

[4] Ibid., 4.

these two exceptions, both from twentieth-century America, are far from typical of Reformed theology.[5]

Returning to the older Reformed thinkers from the generation after the Reformation onward, theologians are virtually unanimously in favor of affirming a covenant between the Father and the Son for the redemption of the world. Early Reformed theologians such as Olevianus, Cocceius, Witsius, and Voetius all affirmed a covenant between the Father and the Son.[6] A short survey of Reformed opinion on the subject shows clearly that it has long been the common view that God entered into a covenant with Christ for the salvation of the elect. Some Reformed theologians have preferred to see two covenants, one between the Father and the Son, usually called the *covenant of redemption*, and another called the *covenant of grace*, agreed upon by the Father and Christ—considered not as the Son, but as the Messiah and representative of the elect. Other Reformed writers prefer to see two aspects to a single covenant. The following survey is certainly not exhaustive, but it offers a glimpse of a few of the best Reformed thinkers.

Caspar Olevianus (1536–1587) may have been the first Reformed theologian to formulate the idea of a pretemporal redemptive covenant between the Father and the Son and the first to use the covenant idea as the organizing principle for systematic theology, which shows how far back historically the notion goes.[7] More importantly, Olevianus apparently was quite conscious of the trinitarian and covenantal link, according to Westminster Seminary Church historian, R. Scott Clark.

> Whether by Heppe or Barth, Olevian has been interpreted primarily as a covenant theologian, but this view needs to be questioned. In fact, Olevian was as much a theologian of the Trinity as he was a federal or covenant theologian. Indeed, he was a federal theologian

---

[5] I am not trying to suggest that these are the only two. There are no doubt others, but these two are well-known.

[6] Heinrich Heppe, *Reformed Dogmatics: Set Out and Illustrated from the Sources,* ed. Ernst Bizer, trans. G. T. Thomson (Grand Rapids: Baker, 1978 [1950]), 376–79.

[7] Lyle D. Bierma, *German Calvinism in the Confessional Age: The Covenant Theology of Caspar Olevianus* (Grand Rapids: Baker, 1996).

because he was a trinitarian theologian. In his mind, to exposit the Trinity, or the ancient trinitarian creeds, was to teach the doctrine of the covenant, since the covenant is nothing more than a way of describing the relations which obtain between the triune God and his elect.[8]

It is perhaps significant that Richard Sibbes (1577–1635), who lectured at Holy Trinity, Cambridge, from 1610–1615 and served as master of Catherine Hall, Cambridge, from 1626 until his death, speaks only of the covenant of grace and includes within it what might be included in the covenant of redemption,[9] whereas his younger contemporary David Dickson (1583–1662), in his famous work *The Sum of Saving Knowledge,* tells us that the Father, Son, and Spirit decree all that comes to pass in time, and then proceeds to expound that decree by the covenants. Man broke the covenant of works, but God in his grace had ordained a way of salvation, the covenant of redemption, "made and agreed upon, between God the Father and God the Son, in the counsel of the Trinity, before the world began."[10] Thus, from very early on, we find both those who refer to two eternal covenants for our salvation (the covenants of grace and redemption) or to only one covenant (the covenant of grace). In either case, the fact that the persons of the Trinity enter into a covenant before the foundation of the world does not change.

Samuel Rutherford (1600–1661), famous for his political treatise *Lex Rex* and for his participation in the Westminster Assembly as one of the prominent representatives from Scotland, wrote a work on the covenant entitled *The Covenant of Life Opened,* in which he distinguishes—upon the basis of the parties of the covenant—between the covenant of grace and the covenant of redemption,

---

[8] R. Scott Clark, "The Catholic-Calvinist Trinitarianism of Caspar Olevian," *Westminster Theological Journal* 61, no. 1 (spring 1999): 16. Note that Clark stops short of what we might expect. He does *not* say, "the covenant is nothing more than a way of describing the relations which obtain among the persons of the Trinity." Assuming that this is a correct exposition of Olevian, we would have to say that his view is typical of Reformed theology in general in that the covenant never quite becomes truly trinitarian.

[9] Richard Sibbes, *The Works of Richard Sibbes* (Edinburgh: Banner of Truth, 1983 [1864]), 6:19 ff. and 464 ff.

[10] David Dickson, *The Sum of Saving Knowledge* <http://www.newblehome.co.uk/dickson/sumss-heads.html>.

which he calls the "covenant of suretyship." The covenant of redemption, according to Rutherford, was a trinitarian covenant.

> It is not the same covenant that is made with Christ and that which is made with sinners. They differ in the subject or the parties contracting. In this covenant of suretyship, the parties are Jehovah God as common to all the three on the one part, and on the other the only Son of God the second person undertaking the work of redemption. In the covenant of reconciliation, the parties are God the Father, Son and Spirit, out of free love pitying us, and lost sinners who had broken the covenant of works. Hence the covenant of suretyship is the cause of the stability and firmness of the covenant of grace.[11]

Thomas Brooks[12] (1608–1680) includes an extended exposition of the covenant of redemption in his treatise "Paradise Opened" (1675).[13] His purpose is pastoral so he does not enter into whatever theological disputes may surround the doctrine in his own day, but he clearly and without much apology differentiates the covenant of grace from the covenant of redemption, offering the usual reasons. One of the distinguishing marks of Brooks's discussion is that he is one of those who explicitly include the Holy Spirit in the covenant. Though in the extended exposition of the covenant and the many Scriptures that he sees as its foundation, he very seldom mentions the Spirit, yet, near the end of the exposition, he mentions that the Spirit of God is involved in the covenant as a "legal witness" and then a little later he writes,

> Consent of all parties, the allowance of the judge, and public record, is as much as can be desired to make all public contracts authentic in courts of justice; and what can we desire more, to settle, satisfy, and assure our own souls that all the articles of the covenant of redemption shall, on all hands, be certainly made

---

[11] Samuel Rutherford, *The Covenant of Life Opened* (Edinburgh: Robert Brown, 1655), 308–309.

[12] Brooks served as preacher before the House of Commons at least on one occasion, December 26, 1648.

[13] In *The Works of Thomas Brooks* (Edinburgh: Banner of Truth, 1980 [1867]) 5:329–403. The subtitle at the top of the page reads appropriately, "The Covenant of Redemption very clearly and largely opened."

good, than this, that these three heavenly witnesses, God the Father, God the Son, and God the Holy Ghost, do all agree to the articles of the covenant, and are all witnesses to the same covenant?[14]

In form, this is a clear statement that the covenant of redemption was a trinitarian covenant, but Brooks does not seem to see the significance of his own point and usually refers to it simply as a covenant between the Father and the Son.

John Owen (1616–1683) distinguishes between the covenant of grace and the covenant of redemption, seeing the latter as the basis for the former.[15] His discussion of the covenant itself is not explicitly trinitarian, but his exposition is evidently the basis for another theologian who argues for a trinitarian approach, John Gill. Gill may have picked up on the following statement or something similar. It does not appear in the discussion of the covenant, but it is obviously relevant.

This, therefore is that which in the first place we shall evince, namely, "That there were from all eternity personal transactions in the holy Trinity concerning mankind in their temporal and eternal condition, which first manifested themselves in our creation."[16]

Thomas Manton (1620–1677) was a Puritan leader and one of the most highly respected ministers of his day. He was appointed as chaplain to Oliver Cromwell, was one of the leading Puritans who helped with the restoration of Charles II, and of all the competent men of his day, the one who was asked to write a commendatory preface to the Westminster Confession and Catechisms. His views on the covenant of redemption are therefore especially interesting from the perspective of the history of Reformed theology.

In his exposition of the covenant of redemption, in addition to including the notion of "decrees" within the covenant, Manton often refers to the Holy Spirit, giving the definite impression that he

---

[14] Ibid., 398.
[15] John Owen, *An Exposition of the Epistle to the Hebrews* (Grand Rapids: Baker Book House, 1980 [1855]), 2:77–97.
[16] Ibid., 43.

regards the covenant as trinitarian.[17] At one point, he says that God's design in the covenant is to "discover the glory of the Trinity."[18] But his most explicit reference to the covenant as trinitarian is the following.

> You have the greatest experience of the love of the Godhead that possibly you could have, that there should be a covenant between the persons of the Godhead, the Father, the Son, and the Holy Spirit, that they would mutually engage one another for your good. It is the highest endearment you could have from them, that God should ordain you his Son to carry on the work of your salvation; therefore engage and give up yourselves to God again: seeing the Lord should devise such a way, and Christ effect it, give up yourselves by covenant to God.[19]

Francis Turretin (1623–1687) refers explicitly to the covenant as trinitarian: "As this work is eternal, it is common and undivided to the whole Trinity with this distinction, however—that each person has his own proper and peculiar mode of operation here, agreeable to this saving economy (1 Pet. 1:2)."[20] He goes on to expound the role of each of the persons of the Trinity in the eternal covenant, affirming that the Father instituted the covenant, the Son executed the covenant, and the Spirit applies the covenant.[21] In addition to offering biblical justification for the notion of a covenant between the Father and the Son, he expounds the "three periods" of the covenant, the first period being "from eternity in the counsel of the most holy Trinity."[22] It is also interesting to note that the only theologians that Turretin mentions as opposing the covenantal paradigm are Socinians, Remonstrants, and Anabaptists.[23]

---

[17] Thomas Manton, *Manton's Complete Works* (Worthington, Penn.: Maranatha Publications, n.d.), 3:368 ff.

[18] Ibid., 388.

[19] Ibid., 386.

[20] Francis Turretin, *Institutes of Elenctic Theology* (Phillipsburg, N.J.: Presbyterian and Reformed, 1992), 2:175.

[21] Ibid.

[22] Ibid., 177–78.

[23] Ibid., 192.

John Flavel (1628–1691) is another famous Reformed theologian who is careful to distinguish the covenants of redemption and grace.[24] Though he speaks in one place as if the covenant included the Holy Spirit,[25] he seems to see it after all as a covenant between the Father and the Son. On the whole, his exposition is pastoral and does not enter into theological details. Thomas Vincent (1634–1678) also offers pastoral instruction in his *The Shorter Catechism Explained from Scripture*.[26] What is significant about this work published in 1674 is that it comes with a recommendation and endorsement by forty ministers, including John Owen, Thomas Manton, Thomas Brooks, and Thomas Watson. Watson (d. 1686) also wrote a work expounding the Shorter Catechism, in which he, in contrast to his friend Vincent, seems to see the covenants of grace and redemption as one.[27]

Herman Wits, known as Witsius (1636–1708), one of the most respected names in the history of Dutch Reformed theology, already in his day denied that the idea of a covenant of redemption was anything like "a new and a late invention," and offers an extended (almost thirty-page) biblical justification and exposition of the covenant. But in Witsius, it is clearly a covenant between the Father and the Son; the Holy Spirit is not mentioned, nor does he speak of it as a trinitarian covenant.[28]

Thomas Ridgeley's (1667–1734) exposition of the covenant of grace is unexceptional. He explains what the word "covenant" means, contrasts the covenant of grace with the covenant of works, and goes through the Scripture passages that support the notion of a covenant between the Father and the Son in eternity.[29] We may note that when he expresses his opinion that the covenant of re-

---

[24] John Flavel, *The Works of John Flavel* (Edinburgh: Banner of Truth, 1968 [1820]), 1:53.

[25] Ibid., 54.

[26] Thomas Vincent, *The Shorter Catechism Explained from Scripture* (Edinburgh: Banner of Truth, 1980 [1674]).

[27] Thomas Watson, *A Body of Divinity Contained in Sermons upon the Westminster Assembly's Catechism* (Edinburgh: Banner of Truth, 1958).

[28] Herman Witsius, *The Economy of the Covenants Between God and Man, Comprehending a Complete Body of Divinity* (Escondito, Calif.: Den Dulk Christian Foundation, 1990), 1:165–192.

[29] Thomas Ridgeley, *Commentary on the Larger Catechism* (Edmonton: Still Waters Revival Books, 1993 [1885]), 440 ff.

demption and the covenant of grace are better viewed as "two great branches of the same covenant" than as two covenants, he says that referring to them as two covenants is "the common mode of speaking."[30] Like John Owen, he is concerned about the idea that the Father and the Son might be thought of as having two different wills, though he does not expound the subject with Owen's subtlety.[31]

Thomas Boston (1676–1732) includes a discussion of the decrees within his exposition of the covenant.[32] Boston specifically asserts that there is no distinction between the covenant of grace and the covenant of redemption. The same covenant is called the covenant of redemption in respect of Christ and the covenant of grace in respect of us. He seems to base his assertion primarily on the words of the Larger Catechism, offering little else in the way of justification for rejecting the common distinction.[33]

After 1650, English and Scottish Reformed theologians largely follow the Westminster Standards, though the question of whether there are one or two covenants is not addressed in them. The Westminster Larger Catechism, in question 31 and its answer, sets forth very simply the idea of a covenant of grace.

> Question 31: With whom was the covenant of grace made?
> Answer: The covenant of grace was made with Christ as the second
> Adam, and in him with all the elect as his seed.

It will hardly be disputed that this was, as Johannes G. Vos says, "made in eternity, before the creation of the world, between God the Father and God the Son," even though the covenant of grace is clearly referred to in questions 30 and 32 as the "second covenant," the covenant of works being first. What this implies is that the covenant of grace was entered into with respect to the condition after the fall, and that it is, therefore, primarily a covenant between God

---

[30] Ibid., 448. The discussion of the covenants of redemption and of grace begins on the previous page where he explains the distinctions between the two covenants.

[31] Ibid., 442–443.

[32] Thomas Boston, *The Complete Works of Thomas Boston*, ed. Samuel McMillan (Wheaton: Richard Owen Roberts, 1980 [1853]), 1:322.

[33] Ibid., 333–34.

and fallen men, with Christ as the mediator—which the theologians of the day usually refer to as the covenant of grace in contrast to the covenant of redemption. The Shorter Catechism in Question 20 implies a covenant of grace in eternity, which might be understood as referring to what is often called the covenant of redemption, but the language is not beyond dispute. The Westminster Confession also refers to the covenant of works as the first covenant and the covenant of grace as the second (VII.2–3). The Westminster Standards, therefore, do not refer unambiguously to a covenant of redemption, even though it does seem to have been commonly held at the time that it was a covenant distinct from the covenant of grace.

John Gill (1697–1771), one of the most brilliant theologians in Baptist history, wrote of the covenant of grace rather than a covenant of redemption, regarding the distinction as an error. But he is very clear and emphatic in his assertion that the covenant of grace is a covenant that concerns the whole Trinity.

> The contracting parties concerned in this covenant, are next to be considered more particularly and distinctly. This covenant is commonly represented as if it was only between the Father and the Son; but I see not why the Holy Spirit should be excluded, since he is certainly promised in it both to Head and members; and in consequence of it, is sent down into the hearts of God's covenant ones, to make application of the blessings, promises, and grace of the covenant to them, and to work a work of grace in them; all which must be by agreement, and with his consent; and I think there are some traces, and some footsteps of all the three persons, as concerned in it, in the dispensation and manifestation of this covenant to the people of Israel (Haggai 2:4,5).[34]

It is also remarkable that Gill goes on to relate the doctrine of the covenant among the persons of the Trinity to our understanding of the Trinity, indicating a tendency in the direction of a more social view.

[34] John Gill, *A Body of Divinity* <http://www.preteristarchive.com/Grace/gillbody.05.html>.

As they are distinct persons, so they have distinct acts of will; for though their nature and essence is but one, which is common to them all, and so their will but one; yet there are distinct acts of this will, put forth by and peculiar to each distinct person: thus their nature being the same, their understanding must be the same; and yet there are distinct acts of the divine understanding, peculiar to each person; the Father knows the Son, and the Son knows the Father, and they have a distinct knowledge and understanding of one another, and the Spirit knows them both, and they know him. And as their nature and essence, so their affections are the same; and yet there are distinct acts of them, peculiar to each person; the Father loves the Son, and has put all things into his hands; the Son loves the Father, and is in all things obedient to him; the Spirit loves the Father and the Son, and they both love him: so their will, though the same, there are distinct acts of it, peculiar to each person; and which appear in their covenanting with each other, and are necessary to it: there is the Father's distinct act of will notified in the covenant, that it is his will and pleasure his Son should be the Saviour of the chosen ones; and there is the Son's distinct act of will notified in the same covenant, he presenting himself, and declaring himself willing, and engaging himself to be the Saviour of them; which distinct acts of the divine will thus notified, formally constituted a covenant between them; and as the holy Spirit dispenses his gifts and grace, the blessings of this covenant, "severally as he will" (1 Co 12:11), this is pursuant to an agreement, to a notification of his will in covenant also.[35]

To Charles Hodge (1797–1878), the evidence for a covenant of redemption, distinct from the covenant of grace, was "clearly revealed in Scripture"[36] since the two covenants have differing parties, promises, and conditions. In Hodge's view, the idea of the three persons of the Trinity making something like a covenant is a great mystery because it seems to challenge the oneness of God when we speak of the Father, Son, and Spirit making a covenant with each other. Hodge's response to this apparent problem is that

---

[35] Ibid.
[36] Charles Hodge, *Systematic Theology* (Grand Rapids: Baker, 1973), 2:359.

the persons to be real persons must be "objective to one another," which includes the idea that "the one may be the object of the acts of the other."[37] He also believes that there are passages of Scripture which are virtually "direct assertions" of the existence of a covenant between the Father and the Son, but he believes that there is a "much wider foundation" for belief in the covenant of redemption found in the fact that the essential elements of a covenant relationship appear in the way the Bible presents the relationship between Father and Son.[38] In Hodge's words, "when one person assigns a stipulated work to another person with the promise of a reward upon the condition of the performance of that work, there is a covenant. Nothing can be plainer than that all this is true in relation to the Father and the Son."[39] The essential elements of the covenant, thus, are "contracting parties, the promise, and the condition."

William G. T. Shedd (1820–1894) agrees with those Reformed theologians who see in Scripture some distinction between a covenant of grace and a covenant of redemption, since there is a difference in the contracting parties to the covenant. In the covenant of grace, the contracting parties are the Father and the elect. In the covenant of redemption, the contracting parties are the Father and the Son. However, this does not mean "that there are two separate and independent covenants."[40] In Shedd's view, "The covenant of grace and that of redemption are two modes or phases of the one evangelical covenant of mercy."[41] While he views the covenant of grace and the covenant of redemption as a single covenant with various aspects, made therefore in eternity, for Shedd, as for Reformed theologians in general, "The first in order is the legal covenant of works. It is founded upon the attribute of justice." This clearly implies that the legal covenant is paradigmatic.

Shedd also points out that although the Westminster standards do not explicitly mention a covenant of redemption in distinction

[37] Ibid., 359–360.
[38] Ibid., 360.
[39] Ibid., 360.
[40] William G. T. Shedd, *Dogmatic Theology* (Minneapolis: Klock & Klock, 1979), 2:360.
[41] Ibid.

from a covenant of grace, they do speak both of a covenant made with the elect (Westminster Confession VII. 3), and of a covenant made with Christ (Larger Catechism, question 31). Within the Westminster Standards themselves, therefore, there is some evidence of what is often represented as two different covenants. More specifically, although some reject the notion of a covenant of redemption, Shedd believes "the weight of authority is in favor of it."

Robert Lewis Dabney (1820–1898) insists firmly on a distinction between the covenant of redemption and the covenant of grace, claiming,

> I hold that this subject cannot be treated intelligibly without distinguishing the covenant existing from eternity between the Father and the Son, from that Gospel promise of salvation on terms of true faith offered to sinners through Christ. . . . The covenant of redemption between the Father and the Son, I hold to be the real covenant transaction, being a free and optional compact between two equals, containing a stipulation which turns on a proper, causative condition, and bearing no relation to time, as it includes no mutable contingency or condition dependent on the uncertain will of creatures.[42]

At the same time, Dabney cautions us to "carefully avoid confusing the subject, by giving to this immanent transaction of the Trinity all the technical features of a 'covenant.'"[43] This word of caution is not directed against the covenantal notion *per se*, but against overly anthropomorphic language in describing the trinitarian relationship, as if "one party produced in the other a willingness to do what he had not previously purposed,"[44] and so forth. Dabney's caution here is grounded in the fact that he sees the covenant as an aspect of intertrinitarian relationship.

A. A. Hodge (1823–1886) describes three views as being common among the Reformed: 1) the covenant of grace was made by God with sinners, Christ being the mediator of the covenant, but

---

[42] Robert L. Dabney, *Lectures in Systematic Theology* (Grand Rapids: Zondervan, 1972), 432.
[43] Ibid., 431.
[44] Ibid.

not one of its parties; 2) there are two covenants for salvation—the covenant of redemption, formed in eternity between the Father and the Son, and the covenant of grace, formed by God with the elect, with Christ as mediator; 3) there is one covenant in eternity between the Father and the Son, the covenant of grace, which embraces the elect in and through Christ since He is their covenant Lord and representative.[45] Hodge himself prefers the third view and regards it as the view of the Westminster Standards, asserting,

> Our Standards say nothing of two covenants. They do not mention the covenant of redemption as distinct from the covenant of grace. But evidently the several passages which treat of this subject (Conf. Faith, ch. vii., para. 3; L. Cat., q. 31; S. Cat., q. 20) assume that there is but one covenant, contracted by Christ in behalf of the elect with God in eternity, and administered by him to the elect in the offers and ordinances of the gospel and in the gracious influences of his Spirit. The Larger Catechism in the place referred to teaches how the covenant of grace was *contracted with* Christ *for* his people. The Confession of Faith in these sections teaches how that same covenant *is administered by* Christ *to* his people.[46]

However, his conception of the covenant as a trinitarian arrangement is emphatic.

> It is evident.—1st. That as God is an infinite, eternal, and immutable intelligence he must have formed, from the beginning, an all-comprehensive and unchangeable Plan of all his works in time, including Creation, Providence, and Redemption.
> 2d. A Plan formed by and intended to be executed in its several reciprocal distributed parts by Three persons, as Sender and Sent, as Principal and Mediator, as Executor and Applier, must necessarily possess all the essential attributes of an eternal Covenant between those persons.[47]

L. Berkhof (1873–1957) is among those who distinguish the covenant of redemption from the covenant of grace, treating each

---

[45] A. A. Hodge, *Outlines of Theology* (Grand Rapids: Zondervan, 1977 [1860]), 369–70.

[46] A. A. Hodge, *The Confession of Faith* (Edinburgh: Banner of Truth, 1958), 126.

[47] *Outlines of Theology*, 367.

in a separate chapter, while at the same time stressing that the two covenants are, in the words he borrows from Shedd, "two modes or phases of the one evangelical covenant of mercy."[48] Like A. A. Hodge, Berkhof clearly delineates the covenant as trinitarian, following Abraham Kuyper's view that the persons of the Trinity in "their internal relations assume the form of a covenant life." The trinitarian covenant is the "archetype of the historical covenants, a covenant in the proper and fullest sense of the word. . . ."[49] At the same time, he is not less clear in following Shedd and the Presbyterian tradition as a whole in seeing the covenant with Adam as the pattern for the covenant of Redemption.[50] He asserts elements of both the Dutch and Scottish approaches—covenant as a form of life and covenant as agreement, respectively—but does not integrate them.

By far the fullest and most helpful discussion of the covenant of redemption and the Trinity is provided by Herman Hoeksema (1886–1965).[51] It deserves more attention than it has been given. To begin with, Hoeksema is perhaps the only twentieth-century theologian who offers in English a significant discussion of Abraham Kuyper's (1837–1920) important insights, though Berkhof obviously had Kuyper in mind when he wrote his chapter on the covenant of redemption. Hoeksema provides an extended quotation from Kuyper indicating that the idea of a covenant between the Father and the Son for the salvation of man must be thought of as pointing to something deeper in the trinitarian life of God. Kuyper may have been the first Reformed theologian to insist that the covenant is theological in the full sense of the word.[52]

What our cursory review of Reformed theology indicates is that Presbyterian theologians considered the idea of a covenant of redemption to be the fount of soteriology. Though they may use the

---

[48] Louis Berkhof, *Systematic Theology*, 4th ed. (Grand Rapids: Baker, 1976), 265.

[49] Ibid., 266.

[50] Ibid., 267.

[51] Herman Hoeksema, *Reformed Dogmatics*, 285–336.

[52] I say "may" simply because there is so much material in Dutch that is not translated into English and I have no idea what other Dutch theologians might have written on the subject. The quotation of Kuyper in Hoeksema does not refer to other theologians, so it may well be that this is Kuyper's original contribution.

word *Trinity* with reference to that covenant, they hardly consider the covenant as anything more than a means to an end. For them, the covenant is an *agreement* that the persons of the Trinity enter into rather than a specific kind of relationship. According to Hoeksema, Kuyper, too, fails to actually get beyond the notion of covenant as a means. Though he thought of the covenant as the essence of the relationship between the persons, he still defined a covenant as an agreement between two parties "over against a third party."[53] But, Hoeksema contends, to consider the covenant an agreement of two parties "over against a third"—which means "over against the power of sin"—is to conceive of the covenant as a *means* rather than a purpose. In Hoeksema's words, "It is a way not a destination." This would mean that when "sin is overcome, the covenant has served its purpose."[54] On these issues, Hoeksema's discussion is penetrating.[55]

Conclusion

Our survey of Reformed material has been superficial and selected, but it suffices to demonstrate that while it is not a uniform view and not usually set forth with emphasis, it is nevertheless quite common for Reformed theologians to view the covenant of redemption as a trinitarian covenant. Among theologians who deny a covenant of redemption, there are some who see the covenant of grace as trinitarian. But even though theologians in the Presbyterian tradition have understood the covenant of redemption or grace to be trinitarian, perhaps without exception they have viewed the trinitarian covenant as a mere agreement entered into in order to respond to the situation of sin. Though their trinitarian language

[53] Ibid., 297.

[54] Ibid.

[55] Less successful, however, is his attempt to establish a distinction between two eternal covenants, one, a covenant between the three persons of the Trinity in which Christ stands as Son, and another, "the counsel of peace," a covenant between the triune God and Christ and those that are given unto Him. If Hoeksema is correct, as I believe that he is, when he asserts that to present the covenant of redemption as if the Holy Spirit is not a party of it is implicitly, even though unintentionally, "a denial of the Trinity," I think that it is also fair to say that Hoeksema's view that the counsel of peace is a covenant between the Trinity and Christ implies an odd and unbiblical separation of the two natures of the second person of the Trinity.

promises something more—as for example when they speak of the love between the persons of the Trinity in reference to the covenant—they never go higher than the notion of the covenant as a means. Dutch theologians Abraham Kuyper and Herman Hoeksema, in contrast with the Presbyterian branch of the Reformed tradition, view the covenant as more than a mere means and take that eternal covenant between the persons of the Trinity as the standard and archetype, the covenantal model. Rather than the covenant of works determining the form of the covenant of redemption, *Kuyper's insight suggests that the trinitarian covenant is the true prototype of every covenant.*

BIBLICAL ARGUMENTS

Just as it is the common faith of the Reformed church to confess the covenants, it is common for dispensational theologians to deride the notions of a covenant of redemption, or one of grace or works. The covenant of redemption, for example, is denounced as "unscriptural and untenable,"[56] and as "a product of theological theory rather than Biblical exposition." Walvoord declares that "the specific formulas of the covenants are inductions from Calvinistic theology which go beyond the Scriptures."[57] Charles Fred Lincoln,

---

[56] Charles Fred Lincoln, "The Development of the Covenant Theory," *Bibliotheca Sacra* 100 (January 1943): 135.

[57] John F. Walvoord, "Millennial Series, Part 7: Amillennial Soteriology," *Bibliotheca Sacra* 107 (July 1950): 285. It is interesting to note that just ten years prior to this article, Walvoord had written, "Major emphasis is usually given the part of the Father and the Son in the eternal covenant, the part of the Holy Spirit being assumed but seldom defined. Both A. A. Hodge and Charles Hodge fail to discuss the part of the Holy Spirit in the covenant of redemption. While the emphasis naturally falls on the part of the Father and the Son, in view of the attention the Scriptures give to these contracting Parties to the covenant, the part of the Holy Spirit in applying the benefits of grace secured through the death of Christ is of great importance and without it the covenant would not be complete. The ministries of the Holy Spirit in the ages are sufficient proof of the importance of this aspect of the eternal covenant. All of the work of the Holy Spirit is related to the purpose of God as contained in the covenant, but certain features of His work are especially significant and may be considered in brief here." He not only assumes that there is a covenant of redemption, he offers help to his Reformed friends in obtaining a properly trinitarian definition! (To add to the irony, see the earlier quotation of A. A. Hodge in this paper in which Hodge clearly outlines the work of the Spirit in the covenant of redemption.) See "The Person of the Holy Spirit, Part 2: The Work of the Holy Spirit in the Old Testament," *Bibliotheca Sacra* 97 (July 1940): 293, as well as "The Person of the Holy Spirit, Part 6: The Work of the Holy Spirit in Salvation," *Bibliotheca Sacra* 98 (July 1941): 292.

one of the early professors at Dallas Seminary, opines, "If the theory were of God, it seems inconceivable that the New Testament should not have made mention of these basic covenants which in covenantism have come to fill the whole horizon of doctrine."[58] More recently, Richard L. Mayhue, Vice President and Dean of the Masters Seminary, finds no explicit mention of a covenant of redemption or a covenant of grace in the Bible and implies that they therefore do not exist. He insists, "Deduced or inferential evidence is not sufficient foundation for something as important as the supposed 'covenant of redemption' or 'covenant of grace.'"[59]

To conclude that the structure of covenant theology is false for the reason that it fails to meet the test for *explicit* mention that dispensational theologians demand is obviously to "win" the argument against covenant theology at too great a cost. It is no wonder that evangelical congregations reared on this sort of reasoning prove easy targets for the cults. If the only truth that the Bible teaches is what it explicitly sets forth, we will be without the doctrine of the Trinity, the very center and heart of the whole Christian religion—a doctrine that is based entirely on inferences and deductions. We would also lose the hypostatic union of Christ's two natures, and dispensationalists themselves might even find it hard to prove the existence of dispensations, to mention only a few doctrines that depend upon inference. Contrary to the modern American demand for explicit statements—in part, the product of a simplistic rationalism that conditions our cultural mentality—the Church all through the ages, in cultures of the East as well as the West, has confessed that the logically necessary implications of Scripture are the teachings of Scripture no less than the explicit

[58] Charles Fred Lincoln, "The Development of the Covenant Theory," *Bibliotheca Sacra* 100 (January 1943): 162. It is interesting to note that Lewis Sperry Chafer was not dogmatically opposed to the idea of a covenant of grace. "Dispensationalism," *Bibliotheca Sacra* 93 (October 1936): 438–439.

[59] Richard L. Mayhue, "Heb. 13:20: Covenant of Grace or New Covenant, An Exegetical Note," *The Masters Seminary Journal* (Fall 1996): 251–257. Though my statements above may sound sharp, I want to emphasize that no disrespect to Dr. Mayhue, or others, is intended. When I attended Grace Theological Seminary with Dr. Mayhue, he was an older student, who encouraged me in my studies as he drove me to our Navy Reserve meetings in Ft. Wayne. I have nothing but the highest regard for him personally. I also believe that he is correct in his understanding of Hebrews 13:20.

statements. However, while we escape the demand for explicit references, it is fair for dispensationalists to demand the biblical grounds for our faith, and given the fact that dispensational theology is so influential in the United States and, through her missionaries, all over the world, it is important to briefly answer that demand and present the biblical reasoning behind the belief in a *trinitarian* covenant.

There are three distinct lines of argument for a belief in a covenant relationship among the persons of the Trinity. First, there is a principle of theology, expressed most famously by Karl Rahner,[60] but antedating his dictum which says that the economic Trinity reveals the ontological Trinity. For our purposes, we need to state the same point more broadly: God works in history in a way that reveals His essential nature. Second, Charles Hodge argued that where the elements of a covenant are found, we also find a covenant. Third, the Gospel of John uses distinctly covenantal language to refer to the relationship between Christ and the Father in a manner that suggests that the covenant relation is basic to the eternal, interpersonal *trinitarian* fellowship. These are the three most important lines of biblical evidence for the doctrine. Associated with these is Abraham Kuyper's argument, referred to above, that if we accept the evidence for what is called a *pactum salutis*, a covenant between the Father and the Son for the salvation of the world, then we must reason from such a notion to a more fundamental covenantal relationship among the persons of the Trinity.

Historical Revelation of the Eternal God

God reveals who He is by His word and by His works. Each is a commentary on the other. Without His works in history, we could hardly understand His word, and without His word, we would

---

[60] Rahner's concern is to find the connection between the Trinity as the doctrine of God and the Trinity as the mystery of salvation. His dictum is, "The 'economic' Trinity is the 'immanent' Trinity and the 'immanent' Trinity is the 'economic' Trinity." Karl Rahner, *The Trinity* (New York: Crossroad Publishing, 1997), 22. It is preferable to state the principle less radically: "The economic Trinity reveals the immanent Trinity."

certainly not be able to fathom the least of His works.[61] If God works in history to reveal Himself, then a careful study of His works is essential to comprehending His written self-revelation. This principle, however, applies with greater force and clarity when we are speaking of God's work in history as it is recorded in Holy Scripture. In Scripture we have not only an inspired record of God's work, but also an inspired theological interpretation so that general historical revelation comes to us integrated with special revelation.

The starting point for such an inquiry cannot be anything other than the biblical account of creation, for the Bible itself emphasizes that how God created the world reveals what kind of a God He is. This is too large a topic to address adequately, but when we consider the Genesis text, certain features stand out. First, what is evident on the surface of the text is that God is a God who creates by command. God addresses the light, which does not yet exist, and commands it to come into being. When it does, He accepts it as good. A similar process continues, until at the end of the sixth day, God blesses all the work He has done.

Now, God obviously could have created the world in other ways, and though we cannot begin to imagine all the possibilities, what we can imagine suggests more than it would be profitable to re-hearse here. The point is, rather, to consider why, of all these possi-bilities, God chose to create the way that He did. What does creation by command mean? First, creation by command may be said to both presuppose and establish a relationship. The command *presupposes* something because God addresses His commands to specific entities, such as light. When God commands the light, it is clear that the light, which does not yet physically exist as light, does exist in the plan of God. God is bringing about His own will

---

[61] See the discussion of natural and special revelation in John Frame, *The Doctrine of the Knowledge of God* (Phillipsburg, N.J.: Presbyterian and Reformed, 1987), 144–48. Also, Cornelius Van Til says, "God's revelation in nature, together with God's revelation in Scripture, form God's one grand scheme of covenant revelation of himself to man. The two forms of revelation must therefore be seen as presupposing and supplementing one another. They are aspects of one general philosophy of history" ("Nature and Scripture," *The Infallible Word*, ed. N. B. Stonehouse and Paul Woolley [Grand Rapids: Eerdmans, 1953], 259).

and plan when He creates by command. The command *establishes* a relationship in the sense that God's command determines His lordship over that which He has commanded. We might say that the very existence of light constitutes a special sort of existence, existence as "being-in-obedience" to the Lord's command. Light is not ontologically primitive. God did not take something already there and bend it to His purpose. Its existence is obedient existence. Needless to say, that is true not just of light but the whole creation.

Second, creation by command leads to a natural covenantal sequence. When there is a command, there is naturally judgment. God looks to see if the light has obeyed His command. Where there is evaluation, there is naturally sanction. God blesses all that He has created. Now, anyone familiar with the Bible will recognize that command, evaluation, sanction is the characteristic covenantal sequence. God the covenant Lord commands the world, which obeys and comes into existence. God looks on what He has created and then blesses the world that He has made. The covenantal progression—command, evaluation and blessing—shows us the relationship between God and the world, reveals to us the way that God works, and shows us what kind of a God the Creator is.[62]

The creation of man bears singular witness to the covenantal character of God, even though the word *covenant* is not specifically used in the creation account. It is clear that man's position is one of representative authority (Gen. 1:26), for which man would have to give account (Gen. 2:15–17). Man is over the world as God's vicegerent, but under God's command and responsible to Him. Man is placed in a position of great blessing, the garden of Eden, the abundant food and beauty of which testifies to its glory. Above all, Eden is the place where man is close to God and in fellowship with Him. When man sinned against God, he faced the covenant

---

[62] Van Til wrote, "Thus every dimension of created existence, even the lowest, was enveloped in a form of exhaustively personal relationship between God and man. The 'ateleological' no less than the 'teleological,' the 'mechanical' no less than the 'spiritual' was covenantal in character" (*Christian Apologetics* [Phillipsburg, N.J.: Presbyterian and Reformed, 1976], 29). Note that Van Til's view of creation as covenantal, frequently expressed in various publications, demands an essentially covenantal approach to the entire Christian worldview.

curse, death. Indeed, the very use of words like "blessing" in the Genesis narrative indicate plainly that man's original position was covenantal,[63] but the whole arrangement is filled with covenantal themes.[64]

Nevertheless, the fact that the story of the creation of man does not explicitly refer to a covenant still bothers some. It should not, for the problem is solved if we simply read further in Genesis, where we do have specific affirmation that Adam was created into a covenantal relationship. When the human race fell and sin grew to the point that God could no longer allow mankind to go on in their sin, God destroyed the world and made a new covenant with Noah. This new covenant unambiguously replicates the relationship between God and Adam. The same language is used (Gen. 9:1–17) and the same commission that was given to Adam is repeated to Noah, when he is told to "be fruitful and multiply and fill the earth" (Gen. 9:1 ff.). If the relationship with Noah is a new beginning for the human race, picking up where Adam's seed left off, so to speak, and if it can be explicitly referred to as a covenant, then it should be evident that the relationship with Adam in the garden was also a covenant.[65]

From the time of Noah onward, the whole history of the Bible is the history of a succession of covenants. Abraham, the children of Israel in Moses' day, David, the Jews in the days of Ezra—all of these people related to God in covenant and there is no other paradigm, no other biblical framework or approach for men to relate to God. Neither is there any single example of God calling a people to be His own except by means of a covenant, nor are there any gaps in the history of the covenants. When the apostle Paul summarizes what may be said of our relationship to God, he subsumes the whole race under either Adam or Christ because covenantal representation determines our eternal destiny (Rom. 5:12 ff.). All of

---

[63] The notion of "blessing," in other words, is distinctly covenantal.

[64] Meredith Kline's *Images of the Spirit* (Grand Rapids: Baker, 1980), 50–56, includes a profound exposition of the covenantal meaning of man as God's image.

[65] See Willian J. Dumbrell, *Covenant and Creation: A Theology of the Old Testament Covenants* (Grand Rapids: Baker, 1984), 15 ff.

this testifies plainly that if history reveals God, it reveals that He is a covenantal God. And if history reveals truth about who God is in Himself, then it reveals that the covenant is something essential to the eternal reality of God. It is precisely this conclusion that is required by the overwhelming predominance of the covenant as the one and only manner of God relating to man and the creation.

If, however, someone insists on denying the notion of a covenantal relationship among the persons of the Trinity, he will have to explain why it is that throughout all of history, pre- and post-fall, that there is no other means of interpersonal relationship between God and man except through a covenant. Where did this covenant idea and reality come from and why does it dominate history so utterly? Unless the opponents of a *trinitarian* covenant can offer reasonable answers to these questions, the weight of presumption falls on the side of those who see God's covenantal work in history as an expression of the fact that He is a covenantal God in eternity, that covenant in history manifests the covenantal nature of the triune God Himself. The compellingly consistent and comprehensive character of God's covenantal relations with the creation and man suggest that the covenant is not a mere secondary feature of the world, but an aspect of God's own being.

Elements of the Covenant

Where we have the elements of a covenant, we have a covenant, as Charles Hodge said, and the principle seems cogent. The plethora of biblical passages quoted by covenant theologians as demonstrating the truth of a covenant between the Father and the Son fall within this category of argument. Two qualifications, however, must be added to the traditional approach. First, of the passages often quoted in support of the covenant of redemption or the covenant of grace, not a few are less than clearly helpful. Theologians like Witsius saw the theme of an eternal covenant in places that we would probably not.[66] Second, as we shall see later, the notion of an

---

[66] I agree with much of Thomas E. McComiskey's criticism of Witsius' use of Scripture. *The Covenants of Promise: A Theology of the Old Testament Covenants* (Grand Rapids: Baker, 1985), 185–88.

agreement is not at all adequate to express the nature of the covenant. Nevertheless, the elements of the agreement idea do point
to God's eternal plan and counsel as covenantal counsel and they
are therefore relevant to the discussion.

Hodge's assertion that the elements of the covenant describe the
relationship between the Father and the Son is confirmed when one
considers the life of Christ, for all the elements of a biblical covenant appear in the gospel accounts of Christ and His relationship
to the Father. This is a strong, even though somewhat indirect argument for a covenant between the persons of the Trinity. For a person who already understands the importance of the covenant in
biblical theology and has learned to recognize covenantal patterns,
the argument is persuasive.[67] The elements of a covenant found in
the eternal relations among the persons of the Trinity usually enun-
ciated include 1) the *parties* to the covenant: at least the Father and
the Son, and often the Spirit, are included; 2) the *conditions* of the
covenant: the giving of a command or commission to Christ before
the foundation of the world; and 3) the *blessing* of the covenant: the
promise of the Father that Christ would be blessed for the work
that He accomplishes.

Every passage which shows that God sent the Son into the world
and that the Father and the Son sent the Spirit into the world implies precreation *trinitarian* counsel.[68] Obviously, God did not decide to send His Son into the world at "the last minute," so to speak.
And the passages that speak of the Father sending the Son must
presuppose the Son's voluntary and joyful submission to the
Father's decree. These verses show us that the Father, Son, and
Spirit together planned the redemption of mankind. But the mere

---

[67] Mayhue complains that many of the passages proposed by covenant theologians as
demonstrations of the covenant only appeal to those who already believe in the covenant theory.
This is partially true and to some degree inescapable. The fact of a hermeneutical circle, however,
does not undermine the argument. It is also true, as I pointed out above, that the older theologians
in particular have been overly enthusiastic in accumulating proof texts.

[68] See John 3:17,34; 4:34; 5:23–24,30,37–38; 6:29,38–40,44,57; 7:16,18,28–29,33;
8:16,18,26,29,42; 9:4; 10:36; 11:42; 12:44–45,49; 13:20; 14:24,26; 15:21,26; 16:5,7;
17:3,8,18,21,23,25; 20:21.

fact of *trinitarian* counsel does not have to be understood as a covenantal plan.

It becomes more obviously covenantal when we see 1) that Jesus (and the Holy Spirit after Him) was commissioned with a specific task; and 2) that His task was not simply a work that He did for Himself, but that He did in a *representative* capacity. Jesus said that it was His food to do the work His Father sent Him to do (Jn. 4:34), that His Father had given Him works to complete (Jn. 5:36), that the Father had given Him commands which He kept (Jn. 14:31; 15:10), and that He glorified the Father by finishing the work the Father gave Him to do (Jn. 17:4). Now, all of these verses—and many more of similar import that could be cited—point to the fact that Jesus had an assigned task. When, we have to ask our dispensational friends, was that task assigned? Was it not before the foundation of the world? Do we not have to think of this as something agreed upon by Father and Son rather than as a task imposed? If the answers to these questions are obvious, so is the covenantal language that is used in reference to this task, especially in John 15,[69] where Jesus applies to the disciples' relationship with Him the language of the covenant from Deuteronomy and borrows the covenantal analogy of the vine tree used in the Old Testament of God's relationship with Israel (cf. Ps. 80:8 ff.; Is. 5:1–7; Jer. 2:21; Ezek. 17:5 ff.). Note that this richly covenantal language not only describes Jesus' relationship with His disciples, but also His relationship with the Father (v. 10).

Romans 5:12–21 shows us very clearly that what Jesus did, He did in a representative capacity. But the notion of representation generates questions such as, Who appoints whom as representative

[69] I will never forget a sermon on John 15 by Dr. S. Herbert Bess, a dispensationalist and one of my professors at Grace Theological Seminary. Dr. Bess showed us that John 15 was replete with Deuteronomic themes and that the language of the passage was covenantal. He was the first person who enabled me to see clearly that obedience to the commandments of God was love to God, according to Deuteronomy and according to Jesus. I remember, young seminarian that I was, rushing up to him afterwards to talk with him. Among other things, I asked the typical dumb seminary boy's question, "How long did it take you to prepare that sermon?" Dr. Bess smiled and answered, "About forty years." His sermon awakened in me both a special interest in the book of Deuteronomy and the theme of the covenant. He was gracious enough to allow me to visit his home some time later and ask further questions about the covenant and he recommended many books and articles on the subject.

and on what basis? What are the stipulations for the representative
and the requirements for those who are to be represented? All of
these and other questions necessarily occur. None can be answered
adequately or biblically apart from the notion of covenant. In other
words, representation implies the structured relationship and arrangements that the Bible calls a covenant. If Jesus functioned as a
representative, then He functioned in covenant. And if that representative status was part of God's eternal plan to save man from
sin, then so was the covenant that it presupposes. To deny this, a
dispensationalist would have to demonstrate that Jesus was not our
representative, or that representation does not imply covenant, or
that salvation was not planned before the foundation of the world.

The third element, reward, is equally clear in Scripture. Jesus'
prayer to the Father suggests that glory was promised Him on the
completion of His work (John 17:4–5) and that the elect are the
love-gift of the Father to the Son (17:24). The apostle Paul tells us
that because Jesus became obedient unto death—clearly suggesting
in this passage a prearranged work that Jesus was sent into the
world to accomplish—the Father "exalted Him and gave Him a
name that is above every name" as a reward and blessing for His
work (Phil. 2:9). The authority that Jesus was given after His resurrection was won by virtue of Jesus having fulfilled the divine commission (Mt. 28:18; Phil. 2:10; Acts 2:36; Rom. 14:9; etc.).
Passages in the Old Testament which speak of the Messiah being re-
warded, such as Isaiah 53:10–12, bear eloquent testimony to the
fact that there was a plan agreed upon by the Father and the Son
long before the incarnation that included the promise of blessing
for the Son.

Now, when the Bible speaks of a relationship in which there is a
hierarchy, responsibility, commands and stipulations, and a promised blessing, the Bible calls that relationship a covenant. There is
much more that could be added to show that the language em-
ployed and the arrangements implied are covenantal in character.
But when the basic issues are so unmistakably apparent, one won-
ders if it is not the dispensationalist here who is entangled in the

web of his own hermeneutical presuppositions. Is it not perhaps the case that in order to escape the implications of an eternal covenant between the persons of the Trinity—presumably because of the theologically pregnant consequences of such a covenant—some dispensationalists forsake the theological methodology of implication, which gave them the doctrine of the Trinity, and flee to the demand for explicit statements?[70] Is this not a counsel of despair?

Covenantal Language

John 17 contains expressions that can only be understood as covenantal language, expressions that not only refer to God's relationship with His people, but that also assert a basic parallel between the covenant that God has with His people and the relationship between the Father and the Son. The obvious implication of this language is that there is a covenant among the persons of the Trinity that serves as analogue and ground for the covenantal relationship that God has with His people.

I have argued for a covenantal interpretation more extensively elsewhere, pointing out first that the context our Lord's prayer suggests the covenantal interpretation.[71]

> [I]n the verses that form the immediate context for Jesus' prayer, the covenantal themes found throughout the Gospel are repeated, a parallel is drawn between Jesus' relationship with the Father and His relationship to the disciples, a famous symbol of Israel's covenant relationship with God is used to describe the relationship of Jesus with the disciples, and, finally, in the symbolic language of the covenant picture, as well as in other parts of the farewell discourse, Jesus uses, with a covenantal significance, various "in" expressions like the ones in His concluding prayer. Once again, then, the ques-

---

[70] As we pointed out above, Lewis Sperry Chafer was willing, though reluctant, to acknowledge a covenant between the persons of the Trinity. "If the term, 'The Covenant of Grace,' refers to an agreement of the three persons of the Godhead between themselves as to the part each would assume in the plan of redemption, as some contend, such an agreement is conceivable, but is not clearly revealed in the Scriptures" ("Dispensationalism," *Bibliotheca Sacra* 93 [October 1936]: 439).

[71] Ralph A. Smith, "Trinity in Covenant," *Christendom Essays* (Niceville, Fla.: Transfiguration Press, 1997), 70–85.

tion is not why we should read the passage covenantally, but how we could possibly read it any other way.[72]

With that covenantal context in mind, I suggested four elements of a covenantal interpretation: "1) the purpose of the prayer as stated in verse 21 and verse 23; 2) the meaning of the glory given to the disciples in verse 22; 3) the idea of unity in verses 21 and 23; 4) the meaning of the "in" phrases."[73] Each of these supports a covenantal interpretation, a simple summary of which is as follows.

> If our interpretation of these four basic issues is correct, the mean-ing of the paragraph in which Jesus prays for the unity of all believ-ers will be something like the following. First, Jesus prays not only for the disciples but also for those who believe through the dis-ciples' preaching (20) in order that they all may be one in covenan-tal faith and obedience (21a).
>
> Second, Jesus takes this to a higher theological plane when He indicates that the covenantal unity of believers has its ground in His dwelling in them and its pattern in the mutual indwelling of the persons of the Trinity (21b, 23a). Christ speaks of a mutual in-dwelling of God and man when He says that believers are to be in God (21b) and He will be in them (23a). This mutuality of ind-welling points to the deep mystery of covenantal fellowship and oneness that comes to fulfillment in the new covenant in Christ.
>
> In the old covenant era, when God made a covenant with Israel to be their covenant Lord, He came to them and dwelt in the tab-ernacle and temple, just as He had originally dwelt with Adam in the garden. This dwelling with man in the old creation was from the beginning a temporary state that pointed forward to the in-dwelling of the Spirit (cf. 1 Cor. 15:20–28, 35–50). In both, the old creation dwelling "with" man and the new creation dwelling "in" man, there is an analogy to the mutual indwelling of the per-sons of the Trinity, not indeed in its ontological meaning, but in its covenantal significance.
>
> Third, Jesus indicates that the purpose of this covenantal ind-welling is the extension of covenant blessing to all the world (21c).

[72] Ibid., 80.
[73] Ibid., 80–83.

Abiding in Christ, the covenant picture of Christians united in Him and bearing fruit through obedience, provides the bridge which links indwelling and the conversion of the world, for when the world sees an obedient Church, it will be converted and the Abrahamic promise will be fulfilled.

Fourth, Jesus speaks of the gift of the glory of God, and the Spirit of glory who glorifies Christ and His people (22). As Jesus taught the disciples shortly before He prayed, it is through the indwelling of the Spirit that Christ and the Father are also present (14:15ff.) and, therefore also, through the Spirit that Christians are one. The same Holy Spirit dwelling "in" all of us, not indeed in any "ontologically" limiting sense, but dwelling in us as He did in the tabernacle, brings all Christians together into one. Through the Spirit, we share the covenant life of God.

Fifth, Jesus implies that His indwelling the Church brings about increased covenantal unity over time ("that they may be perfected in one," 23). There is a process, a covenantal process of pruning the branches so that they bear more fruit, which leads to perfected unity. As the Church matures over time, the world is eventually converted, for it can no longer resist the revelation of the glory of Christ in and through the Church.[74]

The mutual indwelling of the Father and the Son is the pattern for the unity of believers, which can only mean a covenantal unity, for ontological unity among believers in the same way that there may be ontological unity among the persons of the Trinity is unthinkable, and a mere unity of love or fellowship does not do justice to the fact that indwelling is a common covenantal theme, nor to the fact that when the notions of love and fellowship are infused with their most profound biblical meaning, these are words of covenantal relationship.

The Acme of Traditional Reformed Theology

There is also a more narrowly theological argument for a covenantal relationship among the persons of the Trinity, though it

---

[74] Ibid., 83–84.

is based upon the presupposition of a covenant of redemption. The basic thrust of that argument may be seen in Geerhardus Vos's comment on the covenant of redemption as the theological high point of Reformed theology, though Vos does not allow this doctrine to attain its inherent potential. For that we must turn to Abraham Kuyper and Herman Hoeksema. But Vos pointed in the correct direction.

> For it is only in the triune Being that that perfect freedom dominates which the covenant idea appears to demand. Here the covenant is completely two-sided, whereas before the Fall it still had to be regarded as one-sided to the extent that man, as God's subordinate, was in duty bound to act upon the covenant that was proposed. . . .
>
> In the clear light of eternity, where God alone dwells, the economy of salvation is drawn up for us with pure outlines and not darkened by the assistance of any human hand. It is a creation of the triune One from whom, though whom, and to whom are all things.
>
> In the dogma of the counsel of peace, then, the doctrine of the covenant has found its genuinely theological rest point. Only when it becomes plain how it is rooted, not in something that did not come into existence until creation, but in God's being itself, only then has this rest point been reached and only then can the covenant idea be thought of theologically. . . . When it first emerged, the doctrine of the covenant still betrayed the tendency to proceed from man and to survey its surroundings. By the outworking of the doctrine of the counsel of peace this danger was averted and the center placed in God.[75]

On the one hand, it is clear that Vos sees the glory of the covenant of redemption in the fact that it is truly theological, a covenant among the persons of the Trinity in eternity, which does not "proceed from man." Also, the perfect freedom of the covenant and the fully "two-sided" character of the covenant are undeniable.

---

[75] Geerhardus Vos, *Redemptive History and Biblical Interpretation: The Shorter Writings of Geerhardus Vos*, ed. Richard B. Gaffin, Jr. (Phillipsburg, N.J.: Presbyterian and Reformed, 1980), 245–47.

In these respects, the Reformed doctrine of the covenant ascends to the very highest reaches of theological contemplation. On the other hand, however, as much as the covenant of redemption may be exalted as truly theological, it still cannot be denied that the *focus* of the covenant of redemption is man, for it is a covenant to redeem man from sin. In this respect, traditional Reformed theology even at its theological zenith, as expounded by its most profound expositors, *ascends no higher than soteriology*.

There are few exceptions to this imposition of a soteriological ceiling on Reformed theology. Abraham Kuyper was one. Kuyper insisted that the covenant should be understood as fully *trinitarian*.

> If the idea of the covenant with regard to man and among men can only occur in its ectypical form, and if its archetypical original is found in the divine economy, then it cannot have its deepest ground in the *pactum salutis* that has its motive in the fall of man. For in that case it would not belong to the divine economy as such, but would be introduced into it rather incidentally and change the essential relations of the Three Persons in the divine Essence. Besides, the objection arises that the third person of the Holy Trinity in that case remains outside of this covenant and that the Three persons in the eternal Essence are placed in such a relation over against one another that one runs the danger of falling into the error of tritheism. This danger can be escaped only when the divine economy of the Three persons is presented *natura sua* as a covenant relation. . . . We then confess that in the one personality of the divine Essence there consists a three-personal distinction, which has in the covenant relation its unity and an inseparable tie. God Himself is, according to this conception, not only of every covenant, but of the covenant idea as such the living and eternal foundation; and the essential unity [of the Godhead] has in the covenant relation its conscious expression. [76]

Herman Hoeksema criticizes even Kuyper's view as being insufficiently *trinitarian* because, he says, in Kuyper the covenant "is still an agreement" and even "an agreement between two or more

[76] Quoted in Herman Hoeksema, *Reformed Dogmatics*, 295.

parties over against a third party" which would mean that for
Kuyper the covenant "still is means, not purpose."[77] Whether or not
this is altogether fair to Kuyper's conception, it is worth
emphasizing that when we conceive of the covenant as a description
of the *relationship between the persons of the Trinity*, man as such cannot
be the focus of the covenant, nor can the relationship among the
persons of the Trinity be aimed at anything outside of God. When
the covenant is conceived of as an agreement, it is an agreement
about a purpose that the divine persons together seek. Hoeksema,
therefore, defines the covenant as "the bond of God with Himself,"
and he sees its essence as "the communion of friendship" among the
persons of the Trinity.[78] This means, of course, that the covenant
between God and man could be defined as a bond of friendship as
well.

What needs to be added to this is the biblical language and
picture of the covenant. In the Bible, a "bond of friendship" or
"communion" is referred to by the word "love," and love is the
essence of a covenant relationship. The point is worth emphasizing
because the Bible has a lot to say about love that is relevant to our
conception of God and the communion of friendship that
characterizes the *trinitarian* life. The self-denial, humility, seeking
of the honor and glory of the other, commitment, and works that
characterize biblical love are only some of the important aspects of
the covenantal fellowship of Father, Son, and Spirit. Indeed it is
only when we understand that almost wherever the Bible speaks of
love, it speaks of covenant,[79] that we can begin to understand what
it means to say that God is love and to search for the meaning of
that most simple and glorious proposition in the mutual love of the
trinitarian persons.

In addition to this, though Kuyper and Hoeksema are correct, in
my opinion, to say that the notion of the covenant does not attain

---

[77] Herman Hoeksema, *Reformed Dogmatics*, 297.

[78] Ibid., 321–22.

[79] There are not a few exceptions, for the various Hebrew and Greek words for love have a
broad range of use. But love, used in the highest sense of the word, is covenantal—passages that
speak of God's love for the world, the Son's love for the Father, our love to God, and the love that is
required of Christian brethren.

its most essential biblical meaning unless we conceive of it theologically rather than soteriologically, we have to add that it is soteriology—the incarnation of Christ and the love that the Father displays in saving us—that opens the way to our vision of theology. The covenant cannot be confined or restricted to theology proper any more than it can be restricted to soteriology. By understanding that the covenant is the relationship of the persons of the Trinity, we also see its relationship to creation, salvation, and the biblical promise of the future, as well as to the whole Christian worldview. Hoeksema says that the covenant is the end not the means. We ought rather to say that because the covenant is the end, it must also be the means. If the covenant is *trinitarian*, it is comprehensive.

The covenant of redemption, then, is seen to imply a covenant relationship among the persons of the Trinity because it would be odd to imagine a God who knows nothing of covenant in His own nature but who would, upon the presupposition of creation and man's fall, suddenly decide to enter into a covenant to deal with the problems arising from the creation. If, however, the triune God of the Bible is a God in covenant from eternity, not only does the covenant of redemption as a means of dealing with human sin make sense, but the whole biblical doctrine of God and His attributes is seen not as a doctrine which often employs a covenantal analogy to express truth, but as an essentially covenantal truth. The Bible speaks of God in covenantal terms and even suggests a covenant among the persons of the Trinity for the redemption of mankind, because the three persons are perfectly united in the love of the eternal trinitarian covenant. The life of God is covenantal life. God is three persons united in covenantal love.

2

The Character of the Covenant

In our survey of Reformed theology, we saw that confession of a covenant at least between Father and Son, if not among all three persons, is standard. There may be exceptions, but not among the most exceptional Reformed theologians. We have seen some disagreement among these theologians not only on relatively minor issues, but also on the essential issue of the definition of the covenant. Kuyper, and those influenced by him, see the covenant among the persons of the Trinity as an eternal *relationship*, the original covenant, from which all others are defined. The Scottish presbyterian tradition sees the covenant as an *agreement* between the Father and the Son about the salvation of the elect, with the covenant of works as the primary covenant. We have offered evidence suggesting that Kuyper is correct and that the covenantal idea in Reformed theology is in need of revision along Kuyperian lines. The covenant idea must find its ultimate definition in the relationship among the persons of the Godhead. The trinitarian covenant must be foremost, rather than the notions of agreement or treaty. If the covenant is trinitarian, it must be basic to the fellowship of the three eternal persons, not merely something brought in to solve the problem of man's sin.

DEFINING THE COVENANT

If the biblical covenants between men or the covenants that God grants to men are patterned after the divine covenant directly or indirectly, we can look to them to discover the nature of the trinitarian covenant, even though they also may contain elements that would be inappropriate for the trinitarian covenant. Many of the covenants in the Bible, for example, fit into the category of a sovereign disposition, but it is obviously not the case that the covenant among the persons of the Trinity should be thought of as a unilateral imposition.

One of the most outstanding features of the covenants between God and man is the fact that the covenant is a gift from God. God sought Abraham and chose him. The initiative is wholly with God, and the covenant, which points the way to blessing, is itself a blessing. Thus, in the covenant with Abraham, as with later covenants, election and the gift of the covenant are virtually synonymous, a point which comes to explicit and repeated declaration in the law: "For you are a holy people to the LORD your God; the LORD your God has chosen you to be a people for Himself, a special treasure above all the peoples on the face of the earth. The LORD did not set His love on you nor choose you because you were more in number than any other people, for you were the least of all peoples" (Deut. 7:6–7; cf. also Exod. 19:5–6; Deut. 4:37; 10:15; 14:2; 26:18–19; 28:9; etc.). To the elect the covenant is given because God has set His love upon them and it is His purpose to bless them. The covenant begins as the gift of electing love and it teaches the beloved the way to ever richer enjoyment of that love.

The New Testament confirms this when it emphasizes that the requirement of the law is to respond to the loving gift of the covenant with love. Jesus tells us that the essence of the covenant is found in the two most important commandments upon which all the rest hangs, the command to love God and the command to love our neighbor (Matt. 22:37–40). Jesus was not speaking of the law as mere forensic stipulation. He was speaking of the law as God's covenant instruction for His beloved people. Paul repeats Jesus' words when he tells us that the whole law can be summed up in the command to love our neighbor (Rom. 13:10).

When Jesus taught that the covenant is the way to blessing, He defined blessing as love and fellowship. "They who have my commandments and keep them are those who love me; and those who love me will be loved by my Father, and I will love them and reveal myself to them" (Jn. 14:21). Keeping the commands is keeping the covenant. Obedience is love and it wins the blessing of greater fellowship in love. When Christ tells us that if we keep the commandments we will abide in God's love just as He kept the commandments and abode in the Father's love (Jn. 15:10), it is clear that even expressions like "keep the commandments" do not point to a primarily political or legal relationship in the Bible. God is King, but it is our *Father* who is on the throne, and our relationship to Him cannot be narrowly defined in legal terms.

The repeated correlation of love with obedience reminds us that righteousness and love should not be separated in us any more than God's righteousness can be divided from His love. Love and righteousness in God are one, though distinguishable. In the covenant, law is the way of love, and love is righteous and holy.

To define the covenant biblically, we also must take into account the fact that of all the covenants that appear in the Bible, no type of covenant is used to describe the relationship of God with His people with greater frequency or deeper emotion than the marriage covenant. When that relationship is threatened, God's jealousy is depicted as intense passion. Neither Ezekiel nor Hosea is embarrassed by the extreme anthropomorphism involved in such a comparison. As the relationship between Hosea and his wife illustrates, marriage is both a relationship of love and also a structured legal commitment. The contractual aspect of marriage does not detract from its passion, but brings the commitment of love to concrete expression. Hosea loved his wife and apparently forgave her more than once before he finally had to divorce her. Hosea's example was intended to teach Israel that the legal obligations of marriage cannot be broken without destroying the love.

What we see in the covenant is both love and law. James Jordan's definition of the covenant attempts to do justice to both dimensions, "*the covenant is a personal-structural bond which joins the three persons of God in a community of life, and in which man was created to participate*."[1] This can be paraphrased in similar terms to stress that the covenant is a bond of love that structures the community life of the three persons of God. Jordan's definition includes the meaning of the covenant for man also in language that suggests that the covenant is the goal of man's creation and his essential relationship with God, not merely a means. This obviously has eschatological implications.

Jordan's definition also fits nicely with Meredith Kline's observation that for man to be in God's image is to be a covenantal creature. Ancient Near Eastern treaties illustrate only one aspect of the covenant, though they often use words like "love" because they thought of political arrangements in organic terms and in order to emphasize the loyalty demanded by the covenant. But treaties are inadequate as models for understanding the biblical covenants, especially the covenantal relationship of the persons of the Trinity and the gift of God's covenant love to man. If man being God's image is a covenantal fact, then it is broader and deeper than any political analogy alone can depict, though the political analogy should not be regarded as altogether irrelevant either.

What we have seen, then, is that the covenants God gives to man are the expression of His love, in which He takes the initiative as covenant Lord and seeks man's blessing. This is the conception of the covenant that we also find in the Gospels when Jesus speaks of His relationship to the Father. The covenant among persons of the Trinity is a covenant of love in which each of the persons of the Trinity gives Himself wholly to the others, denies Himself to bless the others, and humbles Himself to glorify the others.[2] God's overflowing love was the basis for creating man in His image so that

---

[1] James B. Jordan, *The Law of the Covenant* (Tyler, Tex.: Institute for Christian Economics, 1984), 4 (italics in the original). It should be noted that Jordan's definition of the covenant is trinitarian. The Father is the person *par excellence*, the Son is the Word which structures the covenant, and the Holy Spirit is the personal bond of love.

[2] The expression "covenant of love" seemed good to me as expressing the essence of the relationship among the persons and also as expressing the relationship of Eden. When I first wrote this essay, I was unaware of the book by Clarence Stam, *The Covenant of Love* (Winnipeg: Primier, 2001) and I have still not seen it. I am not sure what his view is, but the view set forth here is not directly related, nor is the language borrowed from him.

man could enjoy covenantal fellowship with God. The original gift of love was given in the very definition of man as God's image. That love is reaffirmed in the plan of redemption. The Bible, therefore, finds covenantal unity in the covenant of love among the persons of the Trinity, an eternal covenant that defines the fellowship of Father, Son, and Spirit and in which man was created to participate.

This does not mean that love is more fundamental than other attributes. On the contrary, all the attributes of God are equally important and each one qualifies and is part of the definition of the others so that we cannot truly understand any one attribute apart from the rest. Righteousness and love are different perspectives on the same covenantal relationship. When we speak of "righteousness," we are focusing on the commandments or stipulations of the covenant. Among the persons of the Trinity, this would mean that each of the persons of the Trinity acts so as to preserve the personal distinctions and boundaries of the persons; none seeks to rob the other of glory or position. "Love" focuses attention on self-sacrificially seeking to glorify and bless the other. But the two terms overlap and point to the same covenantal jealousy to preserve what is right. Love, however, is especially emphasized in Scripture as the summary covenantal attribute. Love is the fulfilling of the whole covenant, the essence of the law.

PERICHORESIS

Catherine M. LaCugna is among those who claim that Augustine's doctrine of the Trinity, as a theology of substance, emphasized the oneness of God to the detriment of God's threeness. In contradistinction to this stands the Greek theology of God, which posits personhood as ultimate and therefore holds a communal view of God that emphasizes the economy of salvation. The Augustinian and Latin view does not deny that God is a God of communion and fellowship, but "speculates on trinitarian communion as an *intra*divine occurrence." Fellowship among the persons of the Trinity is "the unifying force that holds together the three coequal persons who know and love each other as peers." On the Greek view, according to LaCugna, the communion of the persons of the Trinity is to be situated in the economy of redemption so that she can say, "The entire purpose of the economy in the Greek vision is the communion of all in all, all in God, God in all."[3] LaCugna argues that the Greek and Latin theologies offer "two quite different visions of personhood" and that means they also offer different views of the Christian life and Christian society. When we answer the question "Who is God?" we have also answered the questions "Who are we?" and "How shall we live?" This is what makes the doctrine of the Trinity so important.

Kuyper's view of the Trinity suggests a third way, which is a distinctly Reformed contribution to trinitarian theology. Reformed theology can offer and already has offered, even if in an underdeveloped form, a doctrine of God as a God who is "for us" but who remains sovereign, a God who is the model of personhood and society in a concrete and definable manner, but who remains transcendent, a God of love who is close to us, but who is no less Lord and King. The covenant among the persons of the Trinity is Latin in the sense that it is a doctrine of three coequal persons in fellowship, but, insofar as covenant is a concrete idea and the details of our covenant obligation are spelled out in Scripture, it is never abstract. Covenant is also, as Jordan shows, community life, and man was created to enter that community life. In this sense, the Reformed view is also Greek, "the communion of all in all, all in God, God in all," but without the confusion that comes from identifying "in" as expressing an ontological relationship.

Perichoresis is the traditional word to describe the mutual indwelling of the persons of the Trinity.[4] Cornelius Van Til expressed

---

[3] Catherine Mowry LaCugna, *God For Us: The Trinity and the Christian Life* (San Francisco: HarperCollins, 1993), 249.

[4] Since *perichoresis* is a theological word rather than a biblical one, how we define it is less important than how we confess the full doctrine of the Trinity. Perichoresis may be limited to the ontological aspect of the mutual indwelling of the persons of the Trinity and be thought of as the mystery of the three in one, with the notion of covenant coming alongside, in addition to perichoresis. Or perichoresis may be thought of as referring to indwelling in broader terms, which include both covenantal and ontological aspects. In any event, mutual indwelling is both a

this indwelling as the persons of the Trinity being "mutually exhaustive of one another." For Van Til, the mutual indwelling of the persons of the Trinity means the three "have one mind and will" and "a common consciousness."[5] Cornelius Plantinga speaks in similar language:

> Each member is a distinct person, but scarcely an individual or separate person. For in the divine life there is no isolation, no insulation, no secretiveness, no fear of being transparent to another. Hence there may be penetrating, inside knowledge of the other as other, but as co-other, loved other, fellow. Father, Son, and Spirit are 'members one of another' to a superlative degree. . . . There is in the divine life a mysterious, primordial in-ness or oneness relation that is short of a oneness of person but much closer than mere common membership in a class.[6]

Though Plantinga and Van Til do not use the word *covenant*, they are both describing the community life of God that is grounded in the covenantal bond. Their description of that community life is based, at least in part, on the passages in the New Testament that speak of the Father and the Son mutually indwelling one another. When we understand that expressions such as Christ "in" the Father, God "in" us, or we "in" Christ are referring to a covenantal relationship, we see that what is often thought of as ontological is actually covenantal. In God, ontology, the mutual "inness" of the three, is related to an eternal covenant among the persons, but it is not easy to say how. If we say that covenant defines or creates ontology, it seems to suggest that man, by being covenantally united to God, has been or will be metaphysically promoted, which is a fundamentally unbiblical idea. If we say that ontology creates the covenant, it seems to suggest that the covenant is a metaphysical

---

covenantal and an ontological reality, one that provides the divine pattern for covenantal relationships between God and man, and man and man. In this essay, I use *perichoresis* to include covenantal indwelling.

[5] *An Introduction to Systematic Theology* (Phillipsburg, N.J.: Presbyterian and Reformed, 1978), 220.

[6] Cornelius Plantinga, Jr., "The Threeness/Oneness Problem of the Trinity," *Calvin Theological Journal* 23, no. 1 (April 1988): 50–51.

necessity rather than a free commitment of love on the part of the triune persons. We can say, at least, that in God covenant and ontology intersect or share common ground. The equal ultimacy of the one and the many that finds expression in the ontological fact that God is one and three also finds expression in the covenant in which the three so perfectly indwell one another in covenant unity that they share a unity of life so intimate that they may be described as possessing a common consciousness.

For Van Til, the mutually exhaustive representation of the persons in the Trinity is synonymous with the mutual indwelling of the persons of the Trinity, a categorically covenantal idea. Van Til expounded the notion of representation in a manner that implied that God's covenant with man reflects the covenant among the persons of the Trinity.

> It were quite legitimate and true to say that the foundation of all personal activity among men must be based upon the personality of one ultimate person, namely, the person of God, if only it be understood that this ultimate personality of God is a triune personality. In the Trinity there is completely personal relationship without residue. And for that reason it may be said that man's actions are all personal too. Man's surroundings are shot through with personality because all things are related to the infinitely personal God. But when we have said that the surroundings of man are really completely personalized, we have also established the fact of the representational principle. All of man's acts must be representational of the acts of God. Even the persons of the Trinity are mutually representational. They are *exhaustively* representational of one another. Because he is a creature, man must, in his thinking, his feeling and his willing, be representative of God. There is no other way open for him. He could, in the nature of the case, think nothing at all unless he thought God's thoughts after him, and this is representational thinking. Thus man's thought is representative of God's thought, but not exhaustively representative.
>
>   The doctrine of original sin is based upon this purely theistic, because purely biblical, concept of representation. Since the

whole being of God, if we may in all reverence say so, is built upon the representational plan, it was impossible for God to create except upon the representational plan.[7]

In another place, Van Til is quite explicit when he emphasizes that the notion of the persons of the Trinity being mutually representational is the essence of the covenantal idea.

> It may even be said that *Calvin's covenantal idea is Theism come to its own.* The covenant idea is nothing but the representational principle consistently applied to all reality. The foundation of the representational principle among men is the fact that the Trinity exists in the form of a mutually exhaustive representation of the three persons that constitute it. The emphasis should be placed upon the idea of *exhaustion.* This is important because it brings out the point of the complete equality as far as ultimacy is concerned of the principle of unity and of diversity. This mutual exhaustion of the persons of the Trinity places one before the choice of interpreting reality in exclusively temporal categories or in eternal categories. The demand of the doctrine of the Trinity, when thus conceived is that reality be interpreted in exclusively eternal categories inasmuch as the source of diversity lies in the Trinity itself and could never be found in a sense world beyond God. Hence the problem of the one and the many, of the universal and the particular, of being and becoming, of analytical and synthetic reasoning, of the a priori and the a posteriori must be solved by an exclusive reference to the Trinity.[8]

Van Til's emphasis here on the exhaustive nature of the representation of the persons of the Trinity agrees with his statements on the mutual indwelling of the persons of the Trinity; the two are obviously related.[9] Because the persons of the Trinity

---

[7] *A Survey of Christian Epistemology* (Phillipsburg, N.J.: Presbyterian and Reformed, n.d.), 78–79.

[8] *A Survey of Christian Epistemology*, 96. He goes on to say, "It was upon this foundation of a truly trinitarian concept that Calvin built his conception of covenant theology" (97).

[9] See *The Defense of the Faith*, 3rd ed. (Phillipsburg, N.J.: Presbyterian and Reformed, 1967), 25, and *An Introduction to Systematic Theology*, 220 ff.

mutually indwell one another perfectly and wholly, they mutually represent one another. This, according to Van Til, is the essence of the covenant.

In his own way, then, Van Til makes the covenant essential to the nature of the creation, for the world is created to reveal the triune God, and man is God's special representative.[10] If representation is the essence of the covenant and of the doctrine of perichoresis, perichoresis and creation are linked in the theology of Van Til. The covenant in God is the basis for understanding man and the whole creation. Redemption, which restores man to God through covenantal union with Christ, is related to the notion of perichoresis as well.[11]

CONCLUSION

The biblical language of the covenant and the most relevant examples of covenant relationships suggest that it is not adequate to depict the covenant among the persons of the Trinity as an agreement. The marriage relationship, used often as the picture of God's relationship with Israel and the Church, is not a mere agreement for the sake of accomplishing a particular purpose. It is a relationship in which two dwell together as one, give themselves for one another's blessing, and seek one another's honor. It is clearly modeled on aspects of the relationship between Christ and the Father portrayed so beautifully in the Gospels.

The relationships of parent and child, older and younger brother, king and subject, and mutual friends, too, all reflect in various ways the relationship between God and His people, though among these the parent-child relationship, as a created reflection of the Father-Son relationship, has special significance because Adam

---

[10] This observation is relevant to the following discussion of the covenant of works.

[11] In Calvin's theology, the covenantal dimension of the relationships between the persons of the Trinity is not developed and Calvin does not use the word *perichoresis*, but, according to Philip Walker Butin, Calvin's doctrine of the Trinity and the relationship between God and man is an expression of his understanding of the perichoretic indwelling of the three persons. Perichoresis is vital to Calvin's understanding of the Trinity and of our union with Christ by the Spirit. *Revelation, Redemption, and Response: Calvin's Trinitarian Understanding of the Divine-Human Relationship* (New York: Oxford, 1995).

was created as God's son (Luke. 3:38), Israel was God's firstborn (Exod. 4:22), and the people His children (Deut. 14:1). We too are adopted as sons of God (Rom. 8:14–16). Especially in the case of the parent-child relationship, the relationship most obviously modeled after the relationship between the Father and the Son, the notion of "agreement" is patently inappropriate.

Covenant expresses the goal of all creation because man, God's representative and image, is destined to become covenantally one with God, sharing in the fellowship of love that is the life of the Trinity from all eternity. That final covenant conclusion is the realization of the goal of creation. The means to bring about covenantal union between God and man were also of necessity covenantal. Indeed, we can say that in the gift of new covenant salvation, God is projecting the future into the present. The final judgment is over and we are made one with God in Christ. He dwells in us and we in Him. Though we never realize the fellowship of the covenant perfectly in this life because of the remaining influences of sin, it is the very essential truth of salvation. It is what salvation is all about because salvation is restoration—not merely restoration to the original state in Eden, but to the attainment of the goal of Eden.

3

Implications of a Trinitarian Covenant

We have seen that Reformed theology has historically been committed to the notion of a covenant among the persons of the Trinity and that this position is biblically sound, but we have also seen that Reformed theologians have not rendered to this truth its due. No doctrine of theology should be more resonant than one's doctrine of the Trinity. However, Reformed theologians have not offered a distinctly Reformed doctrine of the Trinity in accord with their covenantal insights, nor have they sought to apply the doctrine of the trinitarian covenant more broadly. The reason for this shortcoming is to be found in the fact that in spite of confessing a trinitarian covenant, most Reformed theologians have subordinated the trinitarian covenant to the covenant of works. In doing so, they have impaired their own richest insight into theology proper, subsuming the doctrine of God, as it were, to anthropology and soteriology. Instead of three persons in covenant as the center of the Reformed worldview, the covenant of works became the center of a theological system that has never developed its worldview potential.

Trinity in Covenant as Paradigmatic

What our survey suggests is a revision of Reformed theology in the direction of the principal truth of the Reformed system. This means growth of the center and development of the very essence of Reformed theology, not evisceration. Of the two covenants, the trinitarian covenant and the covenant of works, only one can be the fundamental covenant model.[1] Whichever we choose, the whole of our theology goes with it. If the evidence set forth for a trinitarian covenant is enough to suggest that it is worth rethinking the covenant along trinitarian lines, we cannot avoid rethinking the traditional idea of a covenant of works. Rethinking the covenant of works is imperative from another perspective as well, for the traditional paradigm faces at least three problems inherent in its present structure, two of which are suggested by one of its most zealous defenders, Meredith Kline—which is to say that even those who support the Westminster Standards acknowledge serious problems in their present form.

The Covenant of Works Is Antiquated

First, the covenant of works as traditionally conceived is clearly antiquated because of its notion of merit. The traditional view is defined succinctly in the Westminster Confession as follows.

> 7.1. The distance between God and the creature is so great, that although reasonable creatures do owe obedience unto Him as their Creator, yet they could never have any fruition of Him as their blessedness and reward, but by some voluntary condescension on God's part, which He has been pleased to express by way of covenant.
>
> 7.2. The first covenant made with man was a covenant of works, wherein life was promised to Adam; and in him to his posterity, upon condition of perfect and personal obedience.

The view expressed here implies an outmoded medieval conception of merit. As Lee Irons, a disciple of Meridith Kline, explains, the Westminster doctrine reflects the medieval voluntarist understanding. In the medieval debate about the nature of merit, there were those who insisted that the merit of salvation must be real, the "intellectualist" position that a deed must in strict justice be worthy of the reward (condign merit). Voluntarists, however, sug-

---

[1] I suppose it is hypothetically possible to construct an approach that has a double center, but I am not sure how it would look since the two approaches move in opposite directions.

gested that God was free to consider anything meritorious that He wished to consider meritorious. To reward a deed as meritorious is an arbitrary decision of God, which may be communicated to man by covenantal arrangements (congruous merit).

The doctrine in the Westminster Confession reflects the medieval voluntarist view, for God is said to be infinitely greater than man, so that man cannot do anything, strictly speaking, to merit favor from God, which is to say that on realist grounds, merit is not possible. Thus, the gift of a covenant is God's condescension, a voluntary act of goodness. The covenant that He gave to Adam determines the meaning of merit in the context of the garden. Here we have not only the medieval voluntarist idea of merit, we also have, more specifically, a notion borrowed from the nominalist school of thought and the covenantal thinking of medieval Franciscans.[2] Thus, as Irons shows, the traditional doctrine of the covenant of works is built upon a medieval notion of "merit" that is unbiblical and theologically detrimental.[3]

To revise the traditional theology in a more biblical direction, Irons suggests the following two propositions.

1) Rather than an ontological state intellectually registered in the divine mind, merit is *constituted* only by fulfillment of the stipulations of a divinely sanctioned covenant.

---

[2] See Lee Irons, "Redefining Merit: An Examination of Medieval Presuppositions in Covenant Theology," *Creator, Redeemer, Consummator: A Festschrift for Meredith G. Kline*, ed. Howard Griffith and John R. Muether (Greenville, S.C.: Reformed Academic Press, 2000), 256–62. David Steinmetz points out that, "According to nominalist theology, God enters into covenants that restrict his freedom and that he regards as permanently binding. God could, had he chosen to do so, justify a sinner who lacks an infused habit of grace or refuse to accept a *viator* who has one. The point is that he does not choose to do so *de potentia ordinata*. Having limited himself by his covenant to justify sinners who are infused by a habit of grace, he remains faithful to his decision. The fidelity of God to his covenants *de potentia ordinata* is a central theme of later medieval nominalism. . . . Ideas concerning covenant and promise that seem radical in the fifteenth century were already taught by Cardinal Laborans and his contemporaries in the twelfth century. Indeed, the notion that human merit should be established on the basis of the covenant and promise of God rather than on ontological grounds is a dominant motif if one takes the whole Middle Ages and not merely the thirteenth century into account." *Calvin in Context* (New York: Oxford Univ. Press, 1995), 43–44.

[3] Irons, "Redefining Merit," 253 ff.

(2) The *measure* of merit is defined by the terms of the covenant, which itself is the only possible revelation and definition of divine justice.

There is no such thing as non-covenantal, condign merit because merit is *by definition* constituted by fulfilling what is stipulated in the covenant. And there is no such thing as congruous merit which, since it is covenantal, is supposedly not based on strict justice, because the covenant is *by definition* the revelation of God's justice. Neither merit nor justice exists apart from covenant.[4]

This means that the term *merit* is rescued for theological use by means of a radical redefinition. Merit now means nothing other than "covenant faithfulness"[5]—a perfectly good definition from a biblical perspective, if we understand the persons of God to be in covenant. It is also remarkably similar to the views of N. T. Wright, who claims that "the idea of god's [*sic*] righteousness was inextricably bound up with the idea of the covenant."[6] Wright defines righteousness as "covenant faithfulness."[7] The conclusion that Irons comes to is that the medieval notion of merit is outdated; the word "merit" can be retained only by changing the definition significantly, in accordance with the biblical doctrine of the covenant.

From the perspective suggested in this paper, the redefinition of merit offered by Kline and Irons is perfectly legitimate and its implications significant. One of those implications is that it renders the word *merit* itself unnecessary. If merit simply means "covenant faithfulness," why not dispense with the extra term? The problem for Kline's view is that Kline must be able to relate the definition of righteousness in God's covenant with man to something in God. What is referred to as Euthyphro's dilemma lurks in the shadows of every doctrine of God that does not offer a trinitarian account of divine attributes. As it stands, Kline's view is too close for comfort

---

[4] Ibid., 268.

[5] Irons's expression quoted above is, "fulfillment of the stipulations of a divinely-sanctioned covenant" which can be paraphrased "faithfulness to the covenant."

[6] N. T. Wright, *The New Testament and the People of God* (Minneapolis: Fortress Press, 1992), 272.

[7] Ibid., 271–72.

to the nominalist notion of an arbitrary notion of righteousness, for righteousness is indefinable apart from a covenant between *God and man*.[8]

Another problem raised by Kline's new and more accurate description of the idea of merit in the garden of Eden is as follows: If what is required of Adam in the garden is covenant faithfulness, then the covenant relationship, with all that it implies, is already presupposed. Adam is not earning favor in order to be justified and included in the covenant. Adam is already in covenant. What is required of Adam is simply faithfulness to the relationship already granted, something very different from earning "merit" in order to receive a blessing. But this problem is more a matter of the traditional doctrine not fitting the biblical data, which is our next topic.

The Covenant of Works Is Unbiblical

Second, the traditional doctrine of the covenant of works is unbiblical, an assertion which leads us to the second of the two revisions suggested by Meredith Kline's analysis of the creation narrative. As we saw above, the Westminster doctrine declares that the covenant of works is bestowed upon man *after* he is created by a divine act of "voluntary condescension." Man is not in covenant "naturally" or by virtue of having been created in God's image; rather, the covenant is a post-creation gift to a man whose natural relationship to God is something other than covenantal. In contrast to this doctrine, however, Kline declares,

> It is not the case, as some theological reconstructions would have it, that the covenant was superimposed on a temporally or logically prior noncovenantal human state. The covenant character of the original kingdom order as a whole and of man's status in particular was given along with existence itself.[9]

---

[8] Remember that for Kline, the covenant of works is the *first* covenant.

[9] Meredith Kline, *Kingdom Prologue* (Overland Park, Kans.: Two-Age Press, 2000), 17. See also Kline's *Images of the Spirit*, 55. *Kingdom Prologue,* a helpful work in many respects, is available online at <http://www.two-age.org>.

Irons clarifies more fully:

> [W]e must search for a different footing for the covenant concept
> than it has in its original nominalist context. Therefore, rather than
> making the covenant of works an expression of voluntary conde-
> scension toward unfallen man, it must be regarded as the expres-
> sion of God's justice and goodness toward rational beings created
> in his image and created for eternal Sabbatical enjoyment of God.
> The covenant of works will of necessity now be viewed not as an
> additional structure superimposed on the created order, a created
> order that could very well have existed apart from a covenant rela-
> tionship with the Creator, but as an essential part of God's creation
> of man after his own image. The very act of endowing a rational
> creature with the divine image and thus placing within the very
> constitution of his being a God-created desire for eternal fellow-
> ship and communion with God is an act laden with covenantal
> overtones.[10]

The notion of the covenant as mere means and one which is tied
to the idea of earning merit, essential to the traditional view, stands
in stark contradiction to Kline's understanding of covenant as the
essence of what man is as God's image. Kline's exposition of the
creation narrative has significant implications for the covenant of
works.[11] In the traditional view, the covenant is something bestowed upon man as an act of divine condescension; it is something
added on. From that perspective, the covenant with Adam is *not* essential to our understanding of what it means that he is God's image. He could reflect God's character without being in covenant.
This creates tension because the covenant of works, so central to
the whole theological system, is a nonessential feature of the original relationship in the garden.

Kline's view relieves that tension by making the covenant essential, but then he transfers the tension to another area. If, as
Kline asserts, the medieval notion of merit is outdated and if the

---

[10] Irons, "Redefining Merit," 268.

[11] O. Palmer Robertson agrees with Kline here against the Westminster Standards and offers a
broad overview of the covenant situation in the garden. *The Christ of the Covenants*, 67 ff.

covenant is not something bestowed upon man after creation, but is, rather, a relationship with God that man is created into from the beginning, then it becomes more difficult to conceive of the original relationship as a covenant of works, for the relationship in the garden is an expression of what it means that man is God's image—something that depends upon who the triune God is, not upon a specific plan for Adam. If the covenant is not added to man as a blessing, but rather defines man as God's image, we would think that God's own nature, therefore, must be the standard for the covenant. A temporary relationship in the garden which does not reveal who God is, like the covenant of grace which replaces it, hardly seems the appropriate standard for understanding the image of God. That being the case, we are compelled to look for something in God as the ultimate meaning of covenant. We will return to this subject when we discuss the theological problem with the doctrine of the covenant of works. There are other respects in which we have to say that the traditional view of a covenant of works is unbiblical.

For example, the text of Genesis certainly does not suggest what John Murray includes in his exposition of the "Adamic administration," when he says of the tree of life, "although it was not forbidden as was the tree of the knowledge of good and evil (cf. Gen. 2:16), yet, apparently, by the arrangements of providence or of revelation, it was recognized as reserved for the issue of probationary obedience."[12] Murray's supposition fits perfectly with the notion of a covenant of works, which, as this quotation shows, he denies only in language and not in substance. But the Genesis text records God inviting Adam and Eve to partake freely of all the trees of the garden, the only restriction being that of the tree of the knowledge of good and evil. Since there were only two trees mentioned by name, the prohibition of the one tree was virtually an invitation to the other.[13]

---

[12] John Murray, "The Adamic Administration," *Systematic Theology*, 48.

[13] Why were Adam and Eve in the center of the garden near the tree of the knowledge of good and evil at the beginning of Genesis 3? Was it not because they had come to eat from the tree of life?

It is interesting, however, that Murray's error on this point perfectly expresses what *ought* to be the case in the covenant of works
perspective. If God had granted a covenant of works, then participation in the blessing of the tree of life would have to be suspended
until Adam was justified and his justification would follow his obedience to the command. The progression is: righteousness, justification, life. If the garden situation had been a covenant of works,
the tree of life would have had to be prohibited just as surely as the
tree of the knowledge of good and evil! But it was not.[14] Reformed
theologians usually define the blessing to be earned in the garden as
life, but the Bible shows us that the tree of life was freely available
to Adam and Eve. The blessing to be bestowed was the knowledge
of good and evil, symbolized by the forbidden tree.[15] What could
that mean? It would mean covenantal maturity. If Adam and Eve
had properly responded to the test in the garden, they would have
understood good and evil, and, by having intentionally chosen the
good, confirmed themselves in good.

We see, then, that the whole story of Eden describes a situation
remarkably different from the notion of a covenant of works. God
created man and from the beginning placed him in a position of exalted blessing, giving him freedom to eat of all the trees in the garden, except one. Everything in the garden situation suggests a
perfect paradise, which is why Eden is the model for heaven. As
Kline shows, man is invested with royal-judicial office and glory,
for "to bear the image of God is to participate in the judicial func-
tion of the divine Glory."[16] Man was created a prophet, priest and
king.

---

[14] Of course, the prohibition of the tree of the knowledge of good and evil was not only
probationary, it was also educational, for if Adam and Eve, in the light of the temptation, had
thought about the name of the tree, they should have realized that the temptation to take what was
forbidden contained within it the explanation for the meaning of the tree. The essence of good and
evil was and is simply to trust in God and do what He commands.

[15] Note that according to Deuteronomy 13:1–4, God still tests His people on the essential
question of whether we love Him or not. A false prophet who works signs in the name of some other
god is allowed to come and tempt the people of God. Through the false prophet who brings
forbidden knowledge, God tests His people, just as He tested Adam and Eve in the garden. But the
point of the test is simply "to know whether you love the LORD your God with all your heart and
with all your soul" (Deut. 13:3).

[16] *Images of the Spirit*, 27.

To appreciate the contrast, imagine what a covenant of works *ought* to look like. Since the tree of life symbolizes the ultimate blessing of the covenant, it should be, as Murray thought, strictly forbidden, for to take of the tree of life before they had been justified would be, in effect, attempting to steal heaven—a characteristic feature of pagan religions. But there is more. All of the trees in the garden were symbols of covenant life and blessing and the garden itself was the place of blessing and face-to-face fellowship with God, which *is* life. In the tabernacle and temple, the holy of holies repeats the symbols of the garden, clearly indicating that Adam and Eve began in the innermost sanctuary, the place of highest blessing and life. If the garden itself is the sanctuary and place of blessing, then to truly have a covenant of works, Eden and all its blessings would have to be off limits until Adam and Eve had obtained the merit by which they would be justified and therefore qualified to enjoy the rewards of the covenant. They should be outside the garden sanctuary, working their way in.

But the biblical picture is fundamentally contrary to this. There is no suggestion that Adam and Eve could not be blessed until they acquired merit, however we define the word. Adam and Eve are created as God's image—a covenantal blessing itself—and placed in the original paradise "with God," the highest blessing conceivable in the original creation situation.[17] Rather than the covenant being something that is given to man after creation as a covenant of works that postpones the blessings of life, the covenant in the garden defined a relationship of rich blessing into which Adam was created. The covenant in the garden, therefore, should be seen as an extension of the covenant fellowship of the persons of the Trinity, a covenant of love rather than a covenant of works.

Kline's two basic criticisms of the traditional covenant of works have profound implications. If Adam's relationship with God is by creation a covenant relationship that defines in what ways man is

---

[17] When I emphasize the blessings of the garden, I qualify it by referring to the original situation because it was the plan of God from the beginning to bestow upon man blessings far higher and greater than what he enjoyed in the garden. Not only the original covenant, but also the entire original creation was planned by God to be temporary, as Paul shows us in 1 Corinthians 15.

God's image, and if merit for Adam means "covenantal faithfulness," then what is required of Adam is that he persevere in the covenant by being faithful, living out his faith in God by doing works that correspond with it. In this way, though Adam has no sin nature and is not in a covenant of redeeming grace, he is in a position similar to ours. He is in covenant with God and what is required of him is just perseverance, faithfulness to the covenant. What is required of a Christian? We could say, "To believe! Nothing more, nothing less!" That would be a correct answer, as far as it goes. But we could add, as James did, that faith without works is dead. Adam's problem in the garden was not his theological orthodoxy; it was a problem of orthopraxy. His works were contrary to faith in God. In Adam's case, without the provisions of forgiveness that come with the gospel, one sin brought about the end of the covenant. In our case, because of the death of Christ, we can repent and return unto God when we sin. But the basic situation is still similar. We are required to be faithful to the covenant by having a living faith in God, one that works by love (Gal. 5:6).

By placing Adam in covenant with God and defining merit as faithfulness, Kline has undermined the traditional view of the covenant of works, which requires that the original covenant be a special dispensation of God's kindness that offers, on probation, an opportunity for man to become a full covenant member. John Murray fully appreciated the implications of that scheme and adjusted the situation in the garden to fit that theology by denying that Adam had a right to the tree of life. Kline's view, insofar as he wishes to keep a modified notion of the covenant of works, is a mixed interpretation, but one which points the way to a biblical understanding of Adam as created by God in a covenant of love, a covenant which demanded only that Adam reciprocate God's love.

Speaking of the covenant with Abraham, John Murray makes an important observation about the nature of covenant obedience that applies equally to the covenant with Adam. If we change the word "grace" in the following quotation to "love," we have a perfect description of the Adamic situation, one which accords well with

Kline's suggested revisions to the traditional understanding of the creation covenant.

> The covenant is a sovereign dispensation of God's grace [love]. It is grace [love] bestowed and a relation established. The grace [love] dispensed and the relation established do not wait for the fulfillment of certain conditions on the part of those [Adam and Eve] to whom the grace [love] is dispensed. Grace [love] is bestowed and the relation established by sovereign divine administration. How then are we to construe the conditions of which we have spoken? The continued enjoyment of this grace [love] and of the relation established is contingent upon the fulfillment of certain conditions. For apart from the fulfillment of these conditions the grace [love] bestowed and the relation established are meaningless. Grace [love] bestowed implies a subject and reception on the part of that subject. The relation established implies mutuality. But the conditions in view are not really conditions of bestowal. They are simply the reciprocal responses of faith, love and obedience, apart from which the enjoyment of the covenant blessing and of the covenant relation is inconceivable. In a word, keeping the covenant presupposes the covenant relation as established rather than the condition upon which its establishment is contingent.[18]

The Covenant of Works Is Theologically Inadequate

Third, as we have already suggested, there is a theological problem in the covenant of works doctrine because it reflects a profound inconsistency in the Puritan and Reformed view of the covenant. On the one hand, it is frequently enough observed that the covenant must be an agreement between the persons of the Trinity in eternity, while on the other hand, what is called the covenant of works, made with Adam in the garden, is taken to be the paradigmatic covenant. In other words, the covenant of redemption or grace is defined as a covenant of works for Christ but a gracious

---

[18] John Murray, *The Covenant of Grace* (Phillipsburg, N.J.: Presbyterian and Reformed, 1992), 19. Dr. John M. L. Young gave me a copy of Murray's book when I visited his home in Japan. The passage above further clarified for me the meaning of covenant obedience as loving response rather than "condition" and was instrumental in changing my whole view of the law.

covenant for us. The covenantal idea itself, therefore, is conceived of primarily along the lines of the covenant of works. This is often affirmed by covenant theologians,[19] but by none more explicitly or emphatically than Meredith Kline, who refers to "the eternal intratrinitarian covenant" as "The Father's Covenant of Works with the Son."[20] In Kline's system and in traditional Reformed and Presbyterian theology—the theological system which more than any other seeks to do justice to the sovereign glory of God—we face the profound irony that theology proper has been subordinated to anthropology.

Kline, however, introduced a new and more biblical view of the covenant in the garden when he demonstrated that the covenant in the garden is not added on to some state of nature. Covenant is definitive of man. It is essential to what it means for man to be in God's image. But this necessarily includes the important truth that the idea of a covenant is not that of agreement. What could it mean for man to be in the image of an agreement? Covenant expresses the life of God. For man to be in God's image means to be in the image of the triune God for whom the fellowship of the covenant is His essential being. In other words, if Adam is created into a covenant relationship and if his being the image of God reflects the highest blessings of that covenant relationship—investiture with glory!—then the covenant into which Adam was created ought to be the kind of covenant that characterizes the persons of the Trinity.

Once we see that Kline's view of the covenant eliminates the possibility of a covenant being understood merely as an agreement, we see that the covenant of works can no longer be paradigmatic. The notion would lead to absurdities. What, for example, can it possibly mean for man to be the image of three persons who relate in an eternal covenant of works? Does the Father earn the blessing of the Son and Spirit and vice versa? If Kline's idea of covenant is legitimately applied not merely to an agreement with Adam, but to

[19] See, for example, Robert L. Dabney, *Lectures in Systematic Theology*, 435–36.
[20] Meredith Kline, *Kingdom Prologue*, 21.

the eternal relationships of the persons of the Trinity, are we to understand the mutual earning of covenantal merit to be the essence of their interpersonal relationship? What would it mean for a covenant of works in God to be eternal? How would it reflect the essential fellowship of the Trinity? No doubt Kline would reject this application of his theology, but if the covenant in the garden cannot be properly understood as an agreement, as Kline has shown, then an eternal covenant of works between the Father and the Son could not be simply an agreement about what God will do in history either. It would have to define the very life of God. What Kline offers, then, is a system that cannot be consistently applied.

Consider also that Kline's analysis has made the covenant relationship an essential aspect of man's being, while also claiming that the covenant in the garden is a covenant of works. If for man to be in the image of God means to be in a covenant of works that reflects the eternal covenant of works between the Father and the Son, what do we look forward to in heaven when we will be fully restored as God's image? Shall we look forward to sharing in the eternal covenant of works? What can that possibly mean? Again, Kline can assert that for us to be God's image in heaven does not involve any continuation of a covenant of works, but that seems highly inconsistent with his view that the covenant of works is essential to our being in the image of God. How, why, and when does the definition of the image change?

In the light of these problems, we ought to think of the original covenant as something very different from the traditional covenant of works. What sort of covenant would that be? We have already suggested a covenant of love. Evidence for such a covenantal idea can be found in the covenants that God grants to man, including the most emphatically legal of those covenants, the Mosaic covenant. For even in the Mosaic covenant, we see clearly that the essence of the covenant is love. God loved His people and elected them to be His own (Deut. 7:6–8, etc.), and His one demand from them was to respond to His love with love (Deut. 6:4–5; 7:9–16; 10:12; 11:1, 13, 22; 13:3; 19:9; 30:6, 16, 20; etc.). Yes, they were

the subjects of His kingdom, but they were also His firstborn
(Exod. 4:22), His dearly beloved children (Deut. 14:1) and His
bride (Ezek. 16:1–14). The Mosaic Covenant, too, reflects the relationship between the persons of the Trinity and follows the same
theological paradigm that determines the covenant in the garden.
God is a God of love because He is a covenantal God in whom three
persons are committed to one another in absolute love. When God
creates man as His own image, He does not create a single man
whose definition is to be found through self-contemplation. He
creates a man and a woman who are to love one another. Their
marital love is intended to reflect the covenant love of God. When
they were to have children, they were to love them as God loved
His son Adam.

In this perspective the eternal covenant of love among the persons of the Trinity is the archetypical covenant that determines the
covenant in the garden, rather than a covenant of works in the garden being the pattern for the Trinity. Adam and Eve are immature
and their love has neither been tested nor proved, but they are created as children who naturally respond to the love of their heavenly
Father. Why should their love be tested? So that it may become a
mature love of personal and clear choice, a covenant love of mutual
fellowship. When they sin, however, they reject God's love and pro-
voke His burning jealousy, for love demands love. In the
intertrinitarian fellowship of love, the absolute purity and un-
swerving commitment of the love of the Father, Son, and Spirit
cannot even contemplate, let alone tolerate, infidelity. Adam and
Eve betrayed love. Their sin was an act of treachery. They were
cursed because they broke a covenant of love.

The covenant of love paradigm allows us to see the covenant in
the garden as an expression of God's nature, and it also allows us to
see both the blessing of the covenant and the curse of the covenant
as expressions of the love among the persons of the Trinity. For the
jealousy of each of the persons of the Trinity for the honor of the
others burns with the ardor of absolute love. We should not be sur-
prised if that jealous love comes to expression in an eternal hell

which testifies that Father, Son, and Spirit will not abide whatever betrays love. At the same time, that perfect love also comes to expression in the provision of grace, for the God of love is jealous for His creation. His purpose to bless man and bring man into the fold of the covenantal love of the Trinity cannot be defeated even by man's betrayal. The forgiveness of man's sin upon the basis of the death of God's Son also brings to expression the self-denial and self-giving that are essential to intertrinitarian love. When we make the love of the Trinity, rather than the covenant of works, the covenant standard and model for all biblical covenants, we can revise our understanding of the biblical covenants according to a trinitarian theological model that allows us to acknowledge God as the center of our theology, which is, as Vos suggests, the true genius of Reformed theology.

The Covenant of Works and the Gospel

One objection that may be made to this approach is as follows: To deny the covenant of works is to deny the traditional parallel between Adam and Christ and to undermine the biblical doctrine of justification. Although Meredith Kline has redefined the term "merit" in such a way that we could actually do away with it and use the phrase "covenant faithfulness" instead, he also insists that denial that Adam would have merited eternal life by his obedience is a denial of the gospel. John Murray is faulted for the introduction of a false view of the covenant.

> John Murray's exegetical study of Romans 5 was supportive of the classic doctrine of imputation, but this was undercut by the recasting of covenant theology he undertook in the *Covenant of Grace* (Tyndale Press, 1953). Murray did at least affirm the possibility of meritorious human work, with obedience receiving a just reward, but he limited this to a situation where the reward would perfectly balance the value of the work. (For Murray that meant an obedient Adam must remain in his original state without advancement.) This qualification restricted the possibility to a theoretical moment at the beginning before the covenant was superimposed on

this primal state of nature, since on Murray's (mistaken) definition of covenant, "grace" came with covenant, and that spelled the end of any momentary hypothetical administration of simple justice.[21]

Although Kline is more concerned with Daniel Fuller and Norman Shepherd, he believes that Murray's view of the covenant as essentially a gracious arrangement was the beginning of serious problems in Reformed thinking about the relationship between God and man in the garden. The irony here is that in fact, though Murray did not use the word *covenant* for the relationship between God and man in the garden, his own notion of the Adamic administration fits completely with the covenant of works doctrine. Murray's view is consistent with the traditional covenant of works idea, even though he refused the term, for he denied that Adam had access to the tree of life.

As Kline sees it, denial of the covenant of works undermines the gospel in a rather specific manner.

> Moreover, the parallel which Scripture tells us exists between the two Adams would require the conclusion that if the first Adam could not earn anything, neither could the second. But, if the obedience of Jesus has no meritorious value, the foundation of the gospel is gone. If Jesus' passive obedience has no merit, there has been no satisfaction made for our sins. If Jesus' active obedience has no merit, there is no righteous accomplishment to be imputed to us. There is then no justification-glorification for us to receive as a gift of grace by faith alone.[22]

The claim being made here is rather large: A denial that Adam could have earned the blessing of eternal life in the garden is a denial of the gospel. Kline's statement is not simply that without a covenant of works in the garden, we have no grounds for a doctrine of imputation and therefore no gospel; he goes much further. His claim is that unless our understanding of the covenant of works

[21] Meredith Kline, "Covenant Theology Under Attack," <http://www.upper-register.com/ct_gospel/ct_under_attack.html>.

[22] Ibid.

is that Adam by obedience was able to earn merit, which Kline understands in terms of "strict justice" (as defined by the covenant), we would be implicitly denying the gospel.

But this is certainly not what many, if not most, Reformed theologians have meant by the covenant of works. As may be seen from Irons's critique of the doctrine of merit presupposed in the Westminster Confession, traditional Reformed theology has not been as specific on what it means that Adam could obtain merit. Herman Bavinck—whose writing on the covenant of works was translated by Richard Gaffin for the same festschrift for Meridith Kline in which Irons's article appears—although he is an advocate of the covenant of works doctrine, speaks in precisely the language that Kline condemns.

> In the second place, it is clear that over against God a creature cannot assert or possess a single right. That is impossible by the nature of the case. All that a creature is and has he as such owes to his Creator. Before God he is entitled to nothing; he cannot presume on anything; he has no rights or claims whatsoever. There is never a question of merits [*verdienste*] on the part of the creature before God, and there cannot be; the relation of Creator and creature cuts off every merit of the latter in principle and once for all. That holds true not only after but just as well before the fall. Then, too, man was a creature without claims, without rights, without merits. . . . At the same time, however, the religion of Holy Scripture is such that man can still assert certain rights before God. . . . This is possible simply and solely because God in condescending kindness gives rights to his creature. Every right of creatures is a granted good, a gift of grace, unmerited and nonobligatory. All reward comes from God by grace; neither *meritum de condigno* [condign merit] or *meritum de congruo* [congruent merit] is possible. True religion, therefore, cannot be anything other than a covenant; it has its origin in God's condescending kindness, his grace. Religion bears that character both before and after the fall. . . . Religion is always essentially the same, it only differs in form.[23]

[23] "Herman Bavinck on the Covenant of Works," trans. Richard B. Gaffin, Jr., *Creator, Redeemer, Consummator*, 173–74.

The contrast between Kline and Bavinck is seen even more clearly in the light of Kline's critique of Daniel Fuller.

> Grace is of course the term we use for the principle operative in the gospel that was missing from the pre-Fall covenant. Properly defined, grace is not merely the bestowal of unmerited blessings but God's blessing of man in spite of his *demerits*, in spite of his forfeiture of divine blessings. Clearly, we ought not apply this term *grace* to the pre-Fall situation, for neither the bestowal of blessings on Adam in the very process of creation nor the proposal to grant him additional blessings contemplated him as in a guilty state of demerit. Yet this is what Fuller and company are driven to do as they try to create the illusion of a continuum between the pre-Fall and the redemptive covenants. Only by this double-talk of using the term *grace* (obviously in a different sense) for the pre-Fall covenant can they becloud the big, plain contrast that actually exists between the two covenants (cf. Rom. 4:4).[24]

Fuller's doctrine is not the concern of this essay and no comments on his views are necessary. It is Bavinck's "double talk" that is important here, because it clearly reflects the view of the Westminster Confession. Bavinck sees God's condescension as grace. And he claims that the relationship between Adam in the garden is fundamentally the same relationship to God that men always have because religion is always the same. According to Bavinck, then, the religion of the covenant of works in the garden is not a matter of strict merit, for man can never earn merit in the strict sense of the word. Bavinck does not deny the traditional covenant of works. On the contrary, he expounds it at some length. What he denies with enthusiasm is that Adam could have ever *merited* eternal life—in any sense of the word merit, condign or congruent, strict or loose.

Bavinck is by no means alone in this. His view, rather, is typical of Reformed theologians. Archibald A. Hodge, for example, expounded the covenant of works as a "Covenant of Nature" because

---

[24] "Covenant Theology Under Attack" <http://www.upper-register.com/ct_gospel/ct_under_attack.html>. A modified version appeared in *New Horizons* (February 1994).

it expresses the condition of man in his "natural state," as a "legal covenant" because its condition was conformity to law, as a "covenant of works" because it demanded deeds, and as a "covenant of life" because it promised life. He adds the following:

> It was also essentially a gracious covenant, because although every creature is, as such, bound to serve the Creator to the full extent of his powers, the Creator can not be bound as a mere matter of justice to grant the creature fellowship with himself, or to raise him to an infallible standard of moral power, or to crown him with eternal and inalienable felicity.[25]

Thus, leaving aside more controversial figures such as Daniel Fuller and Norman Shepherd, we ask, has Herman Bavinck denied the gospel? If Kline's narrow formulation of the covenant of works is essential to the gospel, it would seem that he has, together with A. A. Hodge, R. L. Dabney, and many others normally considered to be representatives of the Reformed tradition . But has he denied monergistic grace? There is nothing in Bavinck's formulation of the covenant of works that implies a denial of monergism, which B. B. Warfield considered to be the heart of the gospel.[26] Is there anything in Bavinck's conception that denies the parallel between Adam and Christ, that undermines the notion of two covenant heads in whom are federally included two respective humanities? Again, there is nothing in Bavinck's stated views that would deny

---

[25] *Outlines of Theology*, 310–311. Robert Lewis Dabney, too, writes similarly and uses even more exaggerated "double talk." Grace, for Dabney, is the point of "osculation" between the two covenants! "God's act in entering into a covenant with Adam, if it be substantiated, will be found to be one of pure grace and condescension. . . . God, therefore, moved by pure grace, condescended to establish a covenant with His holy creature, in virtue of which a temporary obedience might be graciously accepted as a ground for God's communicating Himself to him, and assuring him ever after of holiness, happiness, and communion with God. Here then is the point of osculation between the covenant of works and the covenant of grace, the law and the gospel. Both offer a plan of free justification, by which a righteousness should be accepted, in covenant, to acquire for the creature more than he could strictly claim of God; and thus gain everlasting life. . . . But in both [the covenants of works and grace], there was free grace; in both a justification unto life; in both, a gracious bestowal of more than man had earned" (*Lectures in Systematic Theology*, 302).

[26] "The Theology of the Reformation," *Studies in Theology*, vol. 9 of *The Works of Benjamin B. Warfield* (Grand Rapids: Baker, 1981 [1932]), 461–79.

that Adam was the covenant head of the old humanity and Jesus is the covenant head of a new humanity. On the contrary, Bavinck affirms the covenant headship of Adam and Christ. Is there anything in Bavinck's view of the covenant of works that denies the notion of imputation, whether the imputation of Adam's sin to his posterity, or the imputation of His people's sin to Christ, or the imputation of Christ's righteousness to His people? Once again the answer is clearly negative. Bavinck affirms the imputation of Adam's sin to the old humanity, the imputation of His people's sins to Christ, and the imputation of Christ's righteousness to His people.

In the same way that Bavinck's view of the covenant of works, which affirms the gracious character of that covenant, does not contradict or dilute the Reformed conception of the gospel, neither does the idea of a covenant of love. It goes without saying that the monergism of the gospel is in no way diminished. With respect to Adam's condition in the garden, James Jordan expounded a view of the covenant in the garden that follows Kline's insofar as Jordan also sees the covenant as definitive of the original condition and not something added on.[27] We might say that whereas for Bavinck the special grace of the original covenant arrangement is seen in the bestowal of the covenant after creation, for Jordan, the word *grace* may be reserved for the redemptive economy and the notion of condescension to give man a covenant is not the point. Rather God's love is poured out on His creation in the way that love is always bestowed, in covenant. The goodness of God revealed in the garden is that God created man as His image, His beloved son, a status which included his rights to the blessings of the covenant.

Jordan's position agrees with Bavinck and traditional Reformed

[27] See James B. Jordan, "Rebellion, Tyranny, and Dominion in the Book of Genesis," in *Tactics of Christian Resistance,* ed. Gary North (Tyler, Tex.: Geneva Ministries, 1983); "Three 'Falls' and Three Heroes," *Biblical Horizons* 22 (February 1991); "The Dominion Trap," *Biblical Horizons* 15 (July 1990); "Thoughts on Euthanasia and Suicide," *Biblical Horizons* 33 (January 1992); "The Original Low-Down Filthy Male Chauvinist Pig-Dog," *Biblical Horizons* 32 (December 1991); Jeffrey J. Meyers, "Thoughts on the 'Covenant of Works' (Part 1)" and James B. Jordan, "Observations on the Covenant of Works Doctrine," *Biblical Horizons* 52 (August 1993); James B. Jordan, "Thoughts on the 'Covenant of Works' (Part 2)," *Biblical Horizons* 53 (September 1993). All the *Biblical Horizons* articles are available at <http://www.biblicalhorizons.com>.

theology in seeing Adam as on probation as the head of the race.[28] This means, also, that Adam's original position was not the highest possible position but rather that he looked forward to graduating to something better. Where Jordan's and Bavinck's views depart is that in Jordan's view what Adam looks forward to is not the gift of life, but maturity in the covenant—symbolized by the tree of the knowledge of good and evil—which includes confirmation in the blessings of the covenant. In other words, Adam is waiting for the blessings represented by the tree of the knowledge of good and evil. In Bavinck's view and in the thinking of most of Reformed theology, the blessing which Adam lacks is eternal life, which is represented by the tree of life—to which Adam already had access.

For Bavinck and for most Reformed theologians, Adam has transgressed the law and his punishment is a matter of strict law and justice. Jordan's view does not deny law or justice, but focuses on a different and most essential element. Adam's sin is the rejection of God's covenant love. God responds to the sin of man as a holy and offended covenant Lord, Father, and Husband whose love has been subject to the most egregious treachery. It is holy jealousy, which demands the fullest penalty the law can apply, and it is God's gracious love which intervenes to take that penalty on Himself. What is added, however, in no way diminishes from the righteousness of God, for covenant love and law mutually involve and imply one another. God is righteous no less than He is love; both attributes come to expression in the covenant. The legal aspect of the covenant is seen in the structure of the relationship and in the threat of death for disobedience. But this is not "strict justice" in *contradistinction* from love, it is justice fulfilled by love, for betrayed love will seek righteous revenge with jealousy.

Similarly, the doctrine of imputation, including the imputation of Adam's sin on his race, the imputation of His people's sins onto Christ, and the imputation of Christ's righteousness to the redeemed, is in perfect accord with Jordan's view of the original

---

[28] James B. Jordan outlines his view of the "One" covenant and covenant of works in particular in "Thoughts on the 'Covenant of Works' (Part 2)."

Adamic situation. Though Reformed theologians have not come to conclusive agreement on the details of the doctrine of imputation,[29] Kline is correct in affirming that the facts that we are involved in Adam's sin, that our sins were laid upon Christ, and that we are counted as righteous because of His faithfulness to the covenant (Kline's revised view of merit) cannot be denied without denying the gospel. But to affirm these truths, one does not have to agree with Kline's particular formulation of the covenant of works or any other view of the covenant of works.

What Kline insisted upon, however, has not been mentioned. What about the problem of merit? If Adam cannot merit life in the garden, how can Jesus merit life for us in the new covenant? If merit means "covenant faithfulness" and if the covenant defines the standards of righteousness and the promised rewards, it is hard to see how there can be a problem. Was Adam required to be faithful to the covenant in order to be blessed? Yes. Was it such that even one infraction of the covenant meant death? Yes. Was Christ required to be faithful to the covenant in order to be blessed? Yes. Was it such that even one infraction of the covenant would have meant death? Yes. When merit has been redefined as covenant faithfulness and we understand that both Adam and Christ are promised blessings upon the basis of being faithful to the covenant, there seems to be very little lost if we drop the redefined and now unnecessary word "merit."

The difference is that for Kline covenant faithfulness is thought to earn *life*, whereas in Jordan's view, Adam is in covenant with God and enjoys the blessings of life, which are symbolized by the trees and river of the garden and epitomized in Adam's access to the tree of life. What Adam lacked was the knowledge of good and evil, which he needed to obtain in order to fulfill his role as coregent with God. For Adam, therefore, life was not a blessing to be won by merit. Life was essential to the original condition of the covenant. To break the covenant meant death, the loss of Adam's position in

---

[29] John Murray, *The Imputation of Adam's Sin* (Phillipsburg, N.J.: Presbyterian and Reformed, 1979).

the garden. Expulsion from the garden was expulsion from life and the enjoyment of blessing as God's son. In contrast with Adam, Christ comes into the world as a representative of a race of men under the curse and out of the garden. As our representative, He must be faithful to the covenant and die on the cross to win eternal life for us. It is not "merit" that is imputed to us, but a righteous status before God.

What the Bible—and also the Westminster Confession[30]—requires in the way of a parallel between Adam and Christ, then, is not denied on a trinitarian covenant of love approach. None of the essentials—not federal headship, nor the importance of Jesus' active obedience to the demands of the covenant, nor righteousness, nor law, nor imputation—are diminished. Revision of the Westminster Confession and Catechisms along the lines suggested would not entail a contradiction of the theology of the covenant that they teach, nor does it undermine the doctrine of justification by faith. On the contrary, the system of doctrine which finds its genius in the fact that it is wholly theocentric is allowed to attain a mature form, leaving behind the medieval merit system and a doctrine of the covenant that makes the trinitarian covenant subordinate to the covenant of works.

THE DECREE AND THE COVENANT

If the covenant is the bond that joins the persons of the Trinity in a community life, then the decree of God, His plan, and His counsel are all included within that trinitarian fellowship. It is ironic that Hoeksema, who wished to deny that the covenant is a mere means and wanted instead to exalt it as the purpose of all, still held on to the idea of various covenants being made within the Godhead. There is rather one, all- embracing, comprehensive covenant life.

---

[30] The term *covenant of works* in the WCF could be revised to mean simply "a covenant in which obedience is required to the degree that even one sin would bring everlasting condemnation, unless grace intervened," or something similar. But the traditional formula includes so much more and it has been used for so long, that it seems to me better to find other language than to continue with the traditional term. What needs to be emphasized, however, is that the view espoused here in no way denies what is essential to the idea of a covenant relationship with Adam in the garden.

We can isolate various aspects of the covenant life of God and speak of what the Father promised the Son or what the Son was commissioned to do, but we press the point too far when we suggest that the persons of the Trinity have entered into two, three, or more covenants. Some Reformed writers have even described the covenant of grace as the Trinity making a covenant with Christ and the people of God, so that the second person of the Trinity is on both sides of the covenant. It is far better, I believe, to affirm that the covenant defines the fellowship of love in the Trinity, rather than being simply an agreement or a series of agreements.

The debate about infralapsarianism and supralapsarianism is similar. Herman Bavinck offers a solution to this whole debate that expresses also the oneness of God's covenant life.

> [N]either the supra- nor the infralapsarian view of predestination is able to do full justice to the truth of Scripture, and to satisfy our theological thinking. The true element in supralapsarianism is: that it emphasizes the unity of the divine decree and the fact that God had one final aim in view, that sin's entrance into the universe was not something unexpected and unlooked for by God but that he willed sin in a certain sense, and that the work of creation was immediately adapted to God's redemptive activity so that even before the fall, i.e., in the creation of Adam, Christ's coming was definitely fixed. And the true element in infralapsarianism is: that the decrees manifest not only a unity but also a diversity (with a view to their several objects), that these decrees reveal not only a teleological but also a causal order, that creation and fall cannot merely be regarded as means to an end, and that sin should be regarded not as an element of progress but rather as an element of disturbance in the universe so that in and by itself it cannot have been willed by God. In general, the formulation of the final goal of all things in such a manner that God reveals his justice in the reprobate and his mercy in the elect is too simple and incomplete. The "state of glory" will be rich and glorious beyond all description. We expect a new heaven, a new earth, a new humanity, a renewed universe, a constantly progressing and undisturbed unfoldment. Creation and the fall, Adam and Christ, nature and

grace, faith and unbelief, election and reprobation—all together and each in its own way—are so many factors, acting not only subsequently to but also in coordination with one another, collaborating with a view to that exalted state of glory. Indeed, even the universe as it now exists together with its history, constitutes a continuous revelation of God's virtues. It is not only a means toward a higher and richer revelation that is still future, but it has value in itself. It will continue to exert its influence also in the coming dispensation, and it will continue to furnish material for the exaltation and glorification of God by a redeemed humanity. Accordingly, between the different elements of the decree—as also between the facts of the history of the universe—there is not only a causal and teleological but also an organic relation. Because of the limited character of our reasoning powers we must needs proceed from the one or from the other viewpoint; hence, the advocates of a causal world and life-view and the defenders of a teleological philosophy are engaged in continual warfare. But this disharmony does not exist in the mind of God. He sees the whole, and surveys all things in their relations. All things are eternally present in his consciousness. His decree is a unity: it is a single conception. And in that decree all the different elements assume the same relation which *a posteriori* we even now observe between the facts of history, and which will become fully disclosed in the future. This relation is so involved and complicated that neither the adjective "supralapsarian" nor "infralapsarian" nor any other term is able to express it. It is both causal and teleological: that which precedes exerts its influence upon that which follows, and that which is still future already determines the past and the present. There is a rich, all-sided "reciprocity." Predestination, in the generally accepted sense of that term: the foreordination of the eternal state of rational creatures and of all the means necessary to that end, is not the sole, all-inclusive and all-comprehensive, purpose of God. It is a very important part of God's decree but it is not synonymous with the decree. God's decree or counsel is the main concept because it is all-comprehensive; it embraces all things without any exception: heaven and earth, spirit and matter, visible and invisible things, organic and inorganic creatures; it is the single will of God concerning the entire universe with reference to the past, the present, and the future. But predestination concerns the eternal state of rational creatures, and the means thereto: but not all things that ever come into being nor all events that ever happen can be included in these means. Hence, in a previous paragraph we discussed "providence" as a thing by itself, although the relation between it and predestination was clearly shown. In the doctrine of God's decree common grace should receive a much more detailed discussion than was formerly the case, and should be recognized in its own rights. Briefly stated, God's decree together with the history of the universe which answers to it should not be exclusively described—after the manner of infra- and supralapsarianism—as a straight line indicating a relation merely of before and after, cause and effect, means and goal; but it should also be viewed as a system the several elements of which are coordinately related to one another and cooperate with one another toward that goal which always was and is and will be the deepest ground of all existence, namely, the glorification of God. As in an organism all the members are dependent upon one another and in a reciprocal manner determine one another, so also the universe is God's work of art, the several parts of which are organically related. And of that universe, considered in its length and breadth, the counsel or decree of God is the eternal idea.[31]

Bavinck's exposition of the decree functions equally well as an explanation of the covenant. One covenantal relationship of total love, mutual commitment, self-sacrificial giving, and mutual blessing characterizes the life of God and His relationship with the world that He has created, especially including man. God's plan for the world is a covenantal plan, one that includes all that He purposes in history and eternity, a plan that is complex and wonderful beyond our comprehension. In that amazing plan, God Himself determined to become man to save us from our sins, and the three persons of the Trinity devised a covenantal means to rescue the human race from the destruction brought about by man's own sin and folly. God's original purpose to create man for special covenantal

[31] Herman Bavinck, *The Doctrine of God*, trans. William Hendriksen (Edinburgh: Banner of Truth, 1977), 392–394.

fellowship with Himself is realized through the saving work of Jesus Christ, for in Him we are united with God in a covenantal oneness that transcends even the exalted blessedness of Adam's original state.

THE COVENANT STRUCTURE OF THE BIBLE

With Jordan's definition of the covenant, the unity of the biblical doctrine of the covenant in God becomes clear.[32] God is a covenantal God who created the world in covenant with Himself and created man as His special image. When Adam broke the original covenant with God, God graciously renewed the covenant with Adam upon the basis of the future work of Christ. The creation covenant became the "old covenant" so to speak. From the time of Adam onwards, man followed the example of the covenant head in repeatedly breaking the covenant and bringing upon the race the curse of death. But God graciously renewed the covenant also. After Adam, Noah, Abraham, Moses, David, and the restored nation of Israel were granted renewed forms of the covenant, each grounded in the original creation covenant, but each also presupposing and promising the coming of a better covenant. The covenant in Christ is the truly new covenant which places the Church on wholly different grounds. In Christ, the covenant has been fulfilled and the new humanity is now able to live for God and His kingdom by the blessing and power of the Holy Spirit.

Instead of two fundamentally different sorts of covenants, a covenant of strict merit versus a covenant of grace, and instead of a view which requires that the Mosaic covenant be a mixture of merit and grace, the view suggested here is that the covenant in the garden is renewed upon the basis of the new covenant in Christ. Every covenant from the time of the fall is "mixed" in the sense that they are both renewals of the old covenant in the garden and promises of the new. The relationship between works and faith, however, is the

---

[32] Jordan himself has expounded a biblical theology of the covenant, demonstrating the unity and development of the covenant, in his book *Through New Eyes: Developing a Biblical View of the World* (Eugene, Ore.: Wipf & Stock, 1999).

same in every covenant. Works are the manifestation of faith, or in the words of Paul, faith works by love (Gal. 5:6).

The covenants with Adam and Christ are the two covenants around which history moves. In Adam the whole race fell. In Christ, a new race is redeemed. Christ's covenant is parallel to Adam's in many ways, including the demand for true love, utter faithfulness to the covenant. But there are important differences as well, including the fact that Jesus has to pay for the sins of the world in order to redeem the world. The covenant in Christ brings about the fulfillment of the original creation purpose to bring man into covenantal fellowship with God. In Christ, a renewed humanity is one with God and enters the covenantal fellowship of the Trinity. Redemption fulfills the purpose of creation and the biblical story of the covenant comes to a climax in the fellowship of God and man in everlasting covenant love.

Covenant and Eschatology

A covenantal view of God entails a covenantal view of eschatology, if for no other reason simply because our view of God determines everything. More particularly, however, God created man in His own image and gave Adam and Eve a command that implied that the condition of the original creation was immature, though perfect. Man as God's image was created to fulfill the commission: "Be fruitful and multiply; fill the earth and subdue it; have dominion over the fish of the sea, over the birds of the air, and over every living thing that moves on the earth" (Gen. 1:28). This obviously could not be fulfilled by Adam and Eve alone. The whole human race to be born after them participates in the work that God gave to Adam, a work which, at least in part, adds to the definition of the expression "image of God." God is the Creator. Man is a coworker with God who, as God's image, is appointed to "finish" the work of creation, so to speak, by bringing the creation to its full potential. Not just the individual, but also the human race as a whole images God, so that the full meaning of man as God's image is not historically realized until that commission is completed.

Therefore, the notion of man as God's image and the covenantal responsibility given to Adam and his descendents, which was repeated to Noah and his descendents, suggest that a covenantal understanding of man is inescapably eschatological.

Again, we refer to Jordan's definition of the covenant: "*the covenant is a personal-structural bond which joins the three persons of God in a community of life, and in which man was created to participate.*"[33] To say that man was created in God's image is to say that man was created to participate in the covenantal life of God, to fellowship with God. Why, then, should God place the test of the tree of the knowledge of good and evil before Adam in the garden? For the same reason that God gave Adam a test before He gave him a wife. The test was a means of education and maturation. Naming the animals was an easier test, but it also prepared Adam for the second test. The first test taught Adam about his relationship with the other creatures in order to prepare him for his relationship with Eve. The second test was supposed to teach Adam about his relationship with God in order that Adam would be able to enter into mature fellowship with Him and fulfill the task that God had given him in the world.

Though God took the initiative and blessed Adam and Eve, for their relationship with God to be a mature relationship, it was essential that they understand the meaning of that relationship and make a positive choice for it. The test in the garden of Eden placed before the original representative of the race a choice of covenantal love or betrayal. Insofar as it provided Adam the opportunity to affirm God's goodness and say "Yes" to His covenant love, the test was essential for man to become a real covenantal partner, to show understanding of the love of God and respond with love.[34] If Adam had trusted God's word and believed in His love, the test which came through the serpent would have introduced him to the true

---

[33] *The Law of the Covenant* , 4. Italics in the original.

[34] If we consider the test in the garden, it is obvious that it would have been a wholly inadequate response to the temptation for Adam to reject Satan on grounds other than love to God and trust in God (cf. Deut. 13:3). Any response that acknowledged Satan's slander of God's character and denial of God's love would have been giving in to the temptation, even if it did not involve an overt act of disobedience. But, of course, once man gives in to Satan's slander, disobedience is unavoidable.

meaning of good and evil and he would have inherited glory. Adam rebelled instead, but even that did not overturn God's purpose.

This is where eschatology and creation unite. If the fall had been able to overturn God's creation purposes, then Adam's sin would have been Satan's victory against God and the creation. God did not allow His original covenantal purpose for man to be undone by Satan, but devised a means—the incarnation and the cross—whereby man's decision in the garden is taken seriously, while at the same time man may be set free from the otherwise inescapable consequences of that decision. Redemption in Christ is restoration to the original position in the garden and to the commission given to the first Adam, but it is more. In Christ, our position is even higher than it was in the garden, for Christ is both God and man, and in Him we are united to God in the most intimate fellowship imaginable. God and man are one in Jesus and since we are in Him, our covenantal union with God is perfect. The commission of the first Adam was to bring to realization the potential of the physical world around him. But the commission to Christians has another dimension. We are to conquer the world in the name of Christ and for the glory of God. Thus the message of biblical eschatology includes both the horrific consequence of man's sin as well as the truth that Jesus in His death and resurrection defeated Satan, sin, and death. God's creation purpose will be fulfilled by a new humanity which is represented by a new covenant Lord and Head who represents in Himself the union of God and man that was God's original purpose.

This is set forth in the "Great Commission," one of the most often quoted and least understood passages of Scripture. Here Christ called the Church to world conquest in no uncertain terms. He began by announcing that "all authority" had been given to Him, both in heaven and on earth. No more comprehensive claim to authority is imaginable. If words have any meaning, Jesus is King of the world now. Since Jesus already possesses *all* authority in heaven and on earth, there is no more authority for Him to claim. The Church is not being told to wait until He returns before she shares in His rule. Rather, based on the fact of His universal kingship, Jesus commands His disciples to bring all the nations of the world into His kingdom. We translate the words of the commission more literally if we make the word "disciple" into a verb, "Go, therefore, and disciple all the nations."

To be sure, this is not simply a repetition of the original commission in the garden to be fruitful, multiply, and fill the earth. But only the most myopic exegesis could regard it as unrelated. Adam was supposed to fill the earth with his seed. Jesus now commissions His disciples to fill the world with His disciples; every nation is to be converted. All are to be baptized and to be taught to obey all that Jesus commanded. The original commission did not involve spiritual warfare, unless we regard the command to guard the garden as including the notion of warfare against the fallen angels, spirits that Adam would presumably not have known about and who were not fallen at the time the command was given. But the new commission is a call to spiritual warfare, to conquer the world for Christ. As Paul emphasized, our weapons for that warfare are spiritual, not carnal (2 Cor. 10:4; Eph. 6:11–20). Moreover, this conquest is essential to the fulfillment of the promises of salvation given before the coming of Christ in the Abrahamic covenant, which promised that all the families of the world would be blessed through Abraham (Gen. 12:3), and the Davidic covenant, which promised that David's seed would rule the world (Ps. 89:25–28; 22:22–31; Is. 9:6–7; Jer. 23:5; etc.).

Furthermore, the good works that Christians are called to perform extend far more broadly than evangelism, though we should insist that all that a Christian does, insofar as he does it to the glory of God, has evangelistic significance. Works of charity are emphasized in the New Testament. Worship, too, at the very least involves the art of song and the aesthetic aspects of a group coming together before God. The Old Testament tabernacle and temple suggest that a great deal more is involved in a theology of worship. Judicial concerns are essential to the Christian faith, first of all in the life of the Church itself, as Paul clearly explains (1 Cor. 5:1–13), but also

more broadly as well, for the Bible teaches us that magistrates of all
sorts are appointed as servants of God (Rom. 13:1–7). In short,
every lawful kind of labor may be sanctified for the kingdom of
God if it is done in faith and prayer for the glory of God. Technol-
ogy, too, is holy, for however much or often it may be abused and
twisted to unholy purposes, properly applied it extends man's dominion and enables him to glorify God in new and wonderful ways.

The Church, in other words, by making the nations to be
Christ's disciples, brings the human race back to the position of being able to build the kingdom that God called man to build in the
beginning. The New Jerusalem is the Christian vision of the future.
We are seeking a glorious heavenly city. On earth, the Church is to
work for that city until the end of history when the heavenly goal
and the earthly realization come so close that man's historical task
is deemed finished. What the first Adam could not do through his
fleshly seed, the last Adam, through His body, the Church, accomplishes. In this way we see the fulfillment of the eschatological vision implicit in the original covenant and repeatedly confirmed and
expanded in the various covenants of the old covenant era—the
covenants given to Noah, Abraham, Moses, David, and post-exilic
Israel. The last Adam, to repair the damage done by the first and to
bring the human race back to its God-designed destiny, must re-
store man to his covenantal duty. The power of the Holy Spirit,
given on the day of Pentecost, ensures that in this new age, man
will fulfill the will of God for him in history. God and man will re-
joice in the completion of the six-day creation project when the
world is filled with men who praise God and the potential of the
world is brought to its full realization.

Covenantal Worship

Worship in the Bible is a covenantal act, centered on ceremonies
that renew the covenant relationship.[35] It is interesting to note that

---

[35] For a full, profound, and very clear exposition of the Christian worship service, see Jeffrey J.
Meyers, *The Lord's Service: Worship at Providence Reformed Presbyterian Church* (St. Louis, Mo.:
Providence Reformed Presbyterian Church, 1999). A new edition is forthcoming—*The Lord's
Service: The Grace of Covenant Renewal Worship* (Mosow, Idaho: Canon, 2003).

the signs associated with *entrance* to the covenant are never seen to be part of the worship service in Scripture. Circumcision, the sign of the Abrahamic covenant, was applied to sons at the age of eight days (Gen. 17:12; Acts 7:8), apparently in the home. Just as there is no indication that Old Testament circumcision was done in a worship service, in the New Testament also, baptism, rather than being postponed until Sunday worship, was so closely associated with the act of trusting in Christ that it was conducted immediately upon a profession of faith. Perhaps the most striking example of this is the Philippian jailer who, as soon as he and his family believed in Christ, was baptized in the middle of the night (Acts 16:33).

God's gift of the covenant to the nation of Israel at Sinai might be thought of as including a sort of covenant initiation ceremony, for when God appeared on Sinai, the gift of the covenant was celebrated by the covenant meal with Israel's representatives, the elders, on the mountain. The meal was a ratification of the covenant, since the official representatives of God eating the covenant meal before God sealed the covenant, but this was also a "worship service" as well. In the words of John W. Hilber, "In short, the covenant ratification ceremony of 24:1–11 is the concrete description of what YHWH intended as worship. Even the instruction immediately following covenant inauguration in Exodus 24 provides for worshiping YHWH who is present through covenant. Covenant enactment and worship are inextricably linked in a single experience."[36]

Renewal of the covenant was essential to the meaning of the sabbath in ancient Israel, for the sabbath was a sign of the covenant and Israel's keeping the sabbath was required by her relationship with God (Exod. 31:16; etc.). The sabbath was not, as some have thought, simply a day of rest for Israelites to stay home and relax. It was first of all a day of worship, not only for the priests (Lev. 24:5–9; etc.) but also for the people, who were to congregate for worship (Lev. 23:3) and thus keep the covenant (cf. Is. 56:6). The

---

[36] John W. Hilber, "Theology of Worship in Exodus 24," *Journal of the Evangelical Theological Society* 39, no. 2 (June 1996): 179.

weekly sabbath, in fact, was not an isolated sign, but part of a whole
calendar of sabbath festivals and feasts, all of which were times of
holy gathering (Lev. 23:1 ff.) in which the priests presented offer-
ings to renew the covenant (cf. Lev. 2:13; 9:22–23). By contrast,
false worship was breaking the covenant with the true God (Jer.
22:9; etc.) and making a covenant with false gods (Is. 57:8). The
Old Testament connection between covenant and worship is, therefore, clear.

In the New Testament, weekly worship included, or rather centered in, the Lord's Supper (cf. 1 Cor. 11:20), though it was some-
times observed more than once a week (Acts 2:46). It is specifically
said to be a covenantal ceremony: "This is the new covenant in my
blood" (1 Cor. 11:25). It is the New Covenant equivalent of Passover in particular (1 Cor. 5:7), but also of all the festivals and feasts
of the Mosaic covenant, for Christ's death on the cross fulfills them
all. The same connection that the Old Testament makes between
covenant making and false worship is implied by Paul and con-
trasted with the true worship of the Lord's Supper (1 Cor. 10).

But the idea of worship as a covenantal ceremony has a broader
base than just a few passages that speak of worship in the context of
the covenant. The whole worship system of the book of Leviticus
was covenantal, as can be seen when we consider the meaning of
the three sacrifices offered in normal worship in the light of the
biblical order for offering the sacrifices. First, the sin offering was
offered to cleanse the place of worship and open the way for the
worshipper. Then the whole burnt offering was offered as a picture
of the total self-dedication of the worshipper. Finally, there was the
peace offering, which symbolized the fellowship between God and
the worshipper. The tribute or grain offering was the only non-
bloody offering and was offered up with the other sacrifices. The
trespass offering was not part of "regular" worship but was offered
only when the worshipper had committed a specific trespass of the
covenant. In normal worship, the sacrificial sequence included an
act of representative identification between the worshipper and the
animal, in which the worshipper came before God with a sacrifice,

placed his hands on the sacrificial animal, confessed his sins, and then slew the animal. Because the animal was offered as a substitute for the worshipper, he was forgiven and accepted. His status as a covenant member was thus renewed and he was permitted to enjoy the covenant meal of fellowship, the peace offering, which culminated the worship sequence.

Those who refused the sign of the covenant or who refused to renew the covenant would be cut off from the covenant community (Gen. 17:14; Exod. 12:15; 31:14; Lev. 7:20–27; 17:3–4; etc.). Public acts of covenantal disobedience had to be atoned for by the offering of a sacrifice, on pain of losing covenantal status (cf. Lev. 4–5). The same principle applied to the holy nation, which, when she refused to keep the covenant, was cast out of the land (Jer. 17:27; Ezek. 20: 13, 16, 20, 21, 24; 22:28; 23:38; etc.). Thus, for both the individual and the nation, continuity in covenantal status depended on keeping the sabbath and renewing the covenant through the sacrifices. The confession of sin in the sacrificial ritual was essential to forgiveness and renewal, though, of course, godly Israelites could confess their sins outside of the context of the regular sacrifices and they could also offer up special sacrifices whenever they wished. The covenant meal signified the fellowship of the covenant. A portion of the animal that had been offered to God was given back to the worshipper as a gift from God expressing the love and communion of the covenant.

The parallels between the ritual worship of the Mosaic Law and the New Testament ritual of the Lord's Supper are obvious and widely recognized.[37] Just as the purpose of the sacrifices of the law

---

[37] See Anthony C. Thiselton, *The First Epistle to the Corinthians,* The New International Greek Testament Commentary, ed. by I. Howard Marshall and Donald A. Hagner (Grand Rapids and Cambridge: Eerdmans and Paternoster, 2000), 882–86. Thiselton says, "Covenant reflects precisely the major theme which persists from 8:1 to 14:40 . . ." and cites authorities such as W. L. Lane, G. Bornkamm, E. Käsemann, W. Schrage, M. Casey, and E. W. Nicholson among those who interpret the Lord's Supper in the light of the covenant. Needless to say, these men are not all "covenant theologians" operating in terms of a theological bias in favor of seeing the covenant everywhere. The New Testament scholar N. T. Wright may be added to the list of those who see Paul's theology as centered in the covenant. He describes the Last Supper as "a young Jewish prophet, reclining at a table with twelve followers, celebrating a kind of Passover meal, constituting himself and them as the true Israel, the people of the renewed covenant, and doing so in a setting and context which

was the cleansing of the people from sin so that they could continue to live close to God and have Him dwelling among them in
the tabernacle and temple, and included confession of sin and an
implicit or explicit oath to keep the covenant commandments of
God, so also, Christians come to the Lord's Supper in repentance
for sin to renew their oath to God (1 Cor. 11:27 ff.). If we confess
our sins, John teaches, God is *faithful* and *just* to forgive us (1 Jn.
1:9) because He is keeping His covenant promise.

The Lord's Supper, however, is not simply or primarily a ceremony in which we come before God in repentance.[38] As we see
clearly in the sign of the covenant with Noah, covenant signs in the
Bible are first of all signs for God (Gen. 9:12–17). The worshipper
shows the sign of the covenant to God and appeals to Him to be
faithful.[39] The covenant renewal ceremony in which we show the
sign of the covenant unto God, in other words, functions like a
prayer.

But there is more. Worship is not first of all what we offer to
God or do for Him. Worship begins with His invitation. We are
called to worship. Since we are sinners, it is true that confession of
our sins and forgiveness is a prominent aspect of worship, but worship is more than a time of repentance, or Bible teaching, or singing
and prayer. All of these are actually elements in a covenantal fellowship of love. God invites us to come before Him as His bride, the
church. We confess our sins, not because it is important for us to
feel guilty, but because we are open and honest with the God who
loved us so much that He sent His Son to die for us. To sin and fail is
not to betray Him, so long as we are open and honest with Him and
ask Him to forgive our sins. The confession of our sins and the as-
surance that our sins are forgiven is the natural beginning of worship, just as the sin offering in the Mosaic system comes first. When

---

formed a strange but deliberate alternative to the Temple." *Jesus and The Victory of God* (Minneapolis:
Fortress Press, 1996), 437. See also *The Climax of the Covenant: Christ and the Law in Pauline Theology*
(Minneapolis: Fortress Press, 1991).

[38] See Peter Leithart, *Blessed Are the Hungry* (Moscow, Idaho: Canon Press, 2000).

[39] This is true theologically whether or not we choose to follow the exegesis of J. Jeremias who
argues for this as the explicit point of 1 Corinthians 11:23 ff. Cf. J. Jeremias, *The Eucharistic Words of
Jesus,* 3rd ed. (London: SCM, 1966), 252 ff., quoted in Thiselton, *The First Epistle to the Corinthians*,
887–88.

sin is dealt with, the way of fellowship is opened, and the conversation between God and His people can begin. We speak to Him in our prayers and song—for singing in worship is just an exalted form of prayer. He speaks to us in the reading of Scripture and through the message delivered by His servants. The fellowship of love culminates in a meal, as it does also in the Old Testament worship system and as it does in the heavenly Jerusalem in which we come to the marriage feast of the Lamb (Rev. 19:9).

In the covenant meal that we call the Lord's Supper, God testifies to us of His love in Christ. Through His representatives, He gives us the symbols of His Son. The bread and wine do not literally change into the substance of Christ's body and blood, but since they have been appointed by God as the symbols of the covenant, it is the body and blood of Christ that is being offered through the symbols. Though it is through the covenantal representatives of Christ, the elders of the local church, that we receive the bread and wine, it is God the Father who gives us His Son, slain for our sins. In that gift, He says to us that He loves us with an everlasting love. The Father invites us to receive the Son and in so receiving to respond to His love. When we eat the Lord's Supper, we are receiving the gift of God and saying "Yes" to His love.

It is because the Lord's Supper is the gift of His love that God is offended when Christians partake of it unworthily. We are despising His love and grace when we take the Supper lightly. A husband who invites his wife to a special dinner in order to say to her that he loves her is not happy if she refuses to come, or if she comes but pays him no attention, or worse, brings her lover. God's bride is expected to respond to His love—nothing more, nothing less.[40] He invites us to come to His house because He wishes to give to us, to share with us. In the gift of the Lord's Supper, His words of love are made visible and tangible. Our own response is concrete and clear.

---

[40] "And now, Israel, what does the LORD your God require of you, but to fear the LORD your God, to walk in all His ways and to love Him, to serve the LORD your God with all your heart and with all your soul, and to keep the commandments of the LORD and His statutes which I command you today for your good?" (Deut. 10:12–13). Notice how love and obedience to the commandments are equated here as they are in the teaching of Christ in the Gospel of John (14:15; 15:1–16; etc.). John also tells us that love is a necessary sign of faith (1 Jn. 3:10–12).

It is a fitting ceremony for a covenant of love. Whenever we leave
the Lord's Supper out of our worship, we rob ourselves of the testimony of His matchless love and change the character of worship
into something other than family fellowship in which the Father
gives us the covenant sign and professes His infinite love to us.
Worship may then become lecture time, entertainment time, or
counseling time; it may be gaudy and magnificent or it may be
homey and simple; but in any case, without the Lord's Supper, it is
less than the kind of covenantal fellowship that it was designed to
be.[41]

COVENANTAL WORLDVIEW

If the covenant characterizes the very life of the triune God and if it
is the key to all of His relationships with man and the physical universe, then the covenant is the central and most important single
idea in the Christian worldview. This does not mean that the covenant replaces God Himself as the core of Christian truth, for the
persons of the Trinity are united in covenant. What it means is that
the doctrine of the covenant provides the link between the Christian understanding of God as Trinity and every other aspect of the
Christian life. God creates the world and rules it in and by His covenant. He creates man as His covenantal image, so that individual
psychology, racial unity, and social dynamics are fundamentally and
basically covenantal, reflecting the triune creator. Therefore, the
Christian approach to history must—if it is to be true to the Christian doctrine of the Trinity—be covenantal as well. Christians' understanding of the environment and the economy, geometry, law,
politics, the subtleties of metaphysics, the nature of disease, the

---

[41] Peter J. Leithart develops the theology of the sacraments from the nature of the Trinity in an
important article. He briefly summarizes his thesis in these terms: "The argument that follows is
this: God's trinitarian character is the 'very foundation of the possibility,' or the 'foundation of the
inescapability,' of sacraments. Sacraments are not 'exceptions' to God's typically 'non-symbolic'
means of communicating and communing with creatures. Rather, the Creator, because he is Trinity
in Unity and Unity in Trinity, draws his people into fellowship with himself through symbols, of
which the sacraments are a particular kind" ("'Framing' Sacramental Theology: Trinity and Symbol,"
Westminster Theological Journal 62, no. 1 [spring 2000]: 1–16). Leithart's view of the sacraments has
broader implications that touch every aspect of the Christian worldview.

causes of war, and all else under the sun, must be informed by the covenantal perspective, for it is as universally relevant as the triune God who designed and controls all things according to His perfect will. Van Til's covenantal view of perichoresis includes the notion of the three persons mutually representing one another, an idea that offers a trinitarian foundation for a Christian view of the arts.

In the late nineteenth century, Abraham Kuyper issued a call for Calvinists to take on the challenge of presenting their theology as a worldview in response to the non-Christian worldview that had developed since the enlightenment and especially since the dawn of the theory of evolution. But one whole century has passed with very little progress. Cornelius Van Til and his followers have been the primary source of what we might call "worldview Calvinism." R. J. Rushdoony, together with many who were influenced by both him and Van Til, produced numerous books that attempted to set forth the basics of the Christian worldview in the light of Scripture.[42]

Today, followers of Van Til such as John Frame,[43] Vern Poythress,[44]

[42] Rushdoony himself expounded the law of Moses and its application to the modern world in his famous volume, *The Institutes of Biblical Law* (Newark, N.J.: Presbyterian and Reformed, 1973). He also wrote on the history of philosophy (*The One and the Many*), on politics (*The Politics of Guilt and Pity, The American System*), on psychology (*Freud, The Revolt Against Maturity*), and on theology (*Systematic Theology*), just to mention a few of his books and only some of the issues he has discussed. Gary North, Rushdoony's son-in-law, has written on economics. Gary DeMar has written on education and politics. C. Gregg Singer has written on history. George Grant has written on history and contemporary issues. James Jordan has written articles on social and cultural criticism, music, and liturgical renewal. I am not suggesting that any of these men have written the last word on the topics they have covered. What they have done is seriously attempted to apply their Calvinism to issues not normally related to Christian theology. Anyone who wishes to broadly apply Calvinism will have to take these men's work into account, even if he is not persuaded of their approach.

[43] Frame has written primarily on theology and apologetics, but he addresses broader cultural concerns as well. *The Doctrine of God: A Theology of Lordship* (2002); *The Doctrine of the Knowledge of God* (1987); and *No Other God: A Response to Open Theism* (2001); all are published by Presbyterian and Reformed (Phillipsburg, N.J.).

[44] Poythress has written on science and mathematics, as well as linguistics, theology, and biblical interpretation. *Symphonic Theology: The Validity of Multiple Perspectives in Theology* (Phillipsburg, N.J.: Presbyterian and Reformed, 1987); *Science and Hermeneutics* (Grand Rapids: Zondervan, 1988); *The Shadow of Christ in the Law of Moses* (Phillipsburg, N.J.: Presbyterian and Reformed, 1995); "Philosophical Roots of Phenomenological and Structuralist Literary Criticism" and "Ground Rules of New Testament Interpretation," *Westminster Theological Journal* 41, no. 1 (fall 1978): 165 ff. and 190 ff.; "Divine Meaning of Scripture," *Westminster Theological Journal* 48, no. 2 (spring 1986): 241 ff.; "God's Lordship in Interpretation," *Westminster Theological Journal* 50, no. 1 (spring 1988): 27 ff.; "Christ the Only Savior of Interpretation," *Westminster Theological Journal* 50, no. 2 (fall 1988): 305 ff.; etc.

James Jordan, and Peter Leithart[45] all present Christian theology and worldview concerns from a trinitarian and covenantal perspective.

Van Til set forth the basic principle of a worldview that is truly Christian and covenantal when he wrote,

> A truly Protestant view of the assertions of philosophy and science can be self-consciously true only if they are made in the light of the Scripture. Scripture gives definite information of a most fundamental character about all the facts and principles with which philosophy and science deal. For philosophy or science to reject or even to ignore this information is to falsify the picture it gives of the field with which it deals.
>
> This does not imply that philosophy and science must be exclusively dependent upon theology for their basic principles. It implies only that philosophy and science, as well as theology, turn to Scripture for whatever light it has to offer on general principles and particular facts. . . .
>
> Basic to the whole activity of philosophy and science is the idea of the covenant. The idea of the covenant is commonly spoken of in relation to theology alone. It there expresses the idea that in all things man is face to face with God. God is there said to be the world's creator. God is there said to be the one who controls and directs the destiny of all things. But this is tantamount to applying the covenant idea to the philosophic and scientific fields as well as to that of theology. *It is difficult to see how the covenant idea can be maintained in theology unless it be also maintained in philosophy and science. To see the face of God everywhere and to do all things, whether we eat or drink or do anything else, to the glory of God, that is the heart of the covenant idea. And that idea is, in the nature of the case, all inclusive.*[46]

---

[45] Peter Leithart has written on literature and systematic and biblical theology. His literary works include *Brightest Heaven of Invention: A Christian Guide to Six Shakespeare Plays* (Moscow, Idaho: Canon Press, 1996), *Ascent to Love: A Guide to Dante's Divine Comedy* (Moscow, Idaho: Canon Press, 2001), and *Heroes of the City of Man* (Moscow, Idaho: Canon Press, 1999). He has also written a work of biblical and systematic theology that offers a perspective on the kingdom of God that is fundamental to the Christian worldview: *The Kingdom and the Power: Rediscovering the Centrality of the Church* (Phillipsburg, N.J.: Presbyterian and Reformed, 1993).

[46] *Christian Apologetics*, 26. Emphasis added.

Conclusion

The Westminster Confession is in need of revision. Even its most enthusiastic defenders find that they cannot agree precisely with every statement and not a few Presbyterian ministers today question the accuracy of some of its basic theological assertions. To mention a trivial example, is there any Presbyterian minister who really believes that the "covenant of grace is *frequently* set forth in scripture by the name of a testament" as the Westminster Confession of Faith claims (VII.4)? Even though the Confession may be referring to the frequency of the word "testament" in the King James English translation, it only offers four passages as proof texts and the underlying notion of "testament," which must be the point, is only relevant in one context, Hebrews 9:15–17. Virtually all scholars today agree that the word should be "covenant" in most of the cases in which the King James Version rendered the Greek word διαθήκη as "testament."

Minor problems aside, Meredith Kline shows that the Confession is wrong when it speaks of God condescending to give Adam a covenant. Rather, contrary to the Confession, the covenant relationship is essential to what it means that man is God's image, a matter of no little importance in the larger system of theology. Once we recognize that the covenant is not added on to the creation as an act of condescension and that the notion of covenant cannot be limited to an agreement, to continue, as Kline does, to define the covenant in God as a covenant of works—giving theological precedence to the pre-fall covenant—leads to a theologically odd position. The covenant relationship among the persons of the Trinity, which ought to be prior, is modeled after and determined by the covenant in the garden, which is temporally subsequent and ought to be theologically subordinate. If the covenant expresses what it means to be in God's image and if the image of God includes the social as well as psychological aspects of man, then, as Jordan recommends, the trinitarian fellowship of love—a covenant of love—offers much more solid covenantal ground for understanding man and the covenant.

It also offers an approach to revising the Westminster theology that extends the fundamental insight of that theology, develops its full trinitarian potential, and brings its doctrine of God, creation, and salvation into clear relationship. The covenant in God, which Gerhardus Vos considered to be the high point of Reformed theology, is made the central and determining covenant so that the doctrine of the covenant is neither subordinated to anthropology or soteriology, nor so separated from them that it becomes abstract. The covenant of love offers a link between systematic and biblical theology, as well as a trinitarian ground for the whole Christian worldview. As Van Til emphatically stated, the covenant idea is all inclusive because the covenant brings us face to face with the triune God. This is the distinctly Reformed contribution to the doctrine of the Trinity. The systematic concerns of trinitarian and covenant theology, together with the practical concerns of a theology of worship and a presentation of the Christian worldview as a covenantal worldview, can only be unified and comprehensively related when they are all seen to spring from the fountain of a biblically trinitarian theology.